ALSO BY KAY ALLENBAUGH

Chocolate for a Woman's Soul

Chocolate for a Woman's Heart

Chocolate for a Lover's Heart

Chocolate for a Mother's Heart

Chocolate for a Woman's Spirit

Chocolate for a Teen's Soul

Chocolate for a Woman's Blessings

Chocolate for a Teen's Heart

77 STORIES TO TREASURE

AS YOU MAKE

YOUR WISHES COME TRUE

A FIRESIDE BOOK
Published by Simon & Schuster
New York   London   Toronto   Sydney   Singapore

CHOCOLATE
for a
WOMAN'S
DREAMS

KAY ALLENBAUGH

FIRESIDE
Rockefeller Center
1230 Avenue of the Americas
New York, NY 10020

FIRESIDE and colophon are registered trademarks
of Simon & Schuster, Inc.

Manufactured in the United States of America

1   3   5   7   9   10   8   6   4   2

Library of Congress Cataloging-in-Publication Data
Chocolate for a woman's dreams : 77 stories to treasure as
you make your wishes comes true / [compiled by]
Kay Allenbaugh.
p.   cm.
1. Women—Conduct of life.   2. Women—Religious life.
I. Allenbaugh, Kay.
BJ1610 .C528 2001
291.4'32—dc21   2001047410

ISBN 0-7432-1777-2

For information regarding special discounts for bulk purchases,
please contact Simon & Schuster Special Sales at 1-800-456-6798
or business@simonandschuster.com

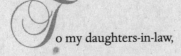

To my daughters-in-law,

Amy and Stephanie:

may all your dreams

come true.

CONTENTS

Introduction   15

I
DREAM WEAVERS

My Wedding-Day Surprise   *Jennifer Dobrenski*   19

Tips for Sweeter Dreaming   *Kay Allenbaugh*   21

Magic Happens   *Mary Zelinka*   23

I Dreamed of Italy   *Gloria Attar*   27

Warm Hands, Warm Heart   *Taylor Joseph*   30

Lucy's Legacy   *Linda Aspenson-Bergstrom*   33

Painted Ladies Rule   *Marilyn D. Davis*   38

This Name's for You   *Beth Boswell Jacks*   41

II
HAPPILY EVER AFTER

I Married a Millionaire   *Lana Robertson Hayes*   47

Confessions of an Addict   *Betty Auchard*   50

A Want-Ad Bonus   *Alicia Wilde Harding*   53

The Sleepwalker   *Eleanor McLaughlin*   57

Queen of the Aisles   *Beverly C. Lucey*   60

Ode to Joy   *Phyllis Jamison*   63

No Place Like Home   *Valentina A. Bloomfield*   67

Under Foot   *Tammy Wilson*   70

III

FAMILY HIGHLIGHTS

Reel Time   *Sande Boritz Berger*   77

Boys and Wheels   *Lana Robertson Hayes*   81

Ashley   *Candis Fancher*   83

A Chinese Business Lunch   *Talia Carner*   86

Finders Keepers   *Rene B. Melton*   89

Whispered Prayers   *Kristi Frahm*   92

Ageless   *Michele Wallace Campanelli*   95

Goodbye, My Son   *Judi Sadowsky*   98

IV

TELLING IT LIKE IT IS

English as a Second Language   *Holly Noelle Schaefer*   103

A Victorious Tug of War   *Beth Duncan*   105

Heating Up the Office   *Melanie Anderson-Caster*   109

Divas! *Sheila Stephens* 113

Life's Not Fair *Felice R. Prager* 115

Adoption Day *Roberta Beach Jacobson* 119

A Picture Is Worth a Thousand Words *Dena McClung* 122

Moments of Truth *Ursula Bacon* 125

V
CREATING A NEW REALITY

Full Throttle *Susan Farr-Fahncke* 131

Cutting Her Losses *LaVonne Holland* 134

Launching a Dream on Lobsters *Barbara Davey* 137

In the Twilight Zone *Margo Ballantyne* 139

Doing College Again—My Way *Betsy Humphreys* 142

I Temped for the Vatican *Linda H. Waterman* 145

The Mentor *Mitzi Chandler* 148

Memories and Modeling *Catherine Vaughan-Obregon* 151

VI
KIDS ARE TEACHERS, TOO

Prying Eyes *Shelley Sigman* 159

A Walk by Faith *Kathie Harrington* 162

Cannonball! *Debra Ayers Brown* 165

Sophia and the Boom-Boom-Boom   *Carol L. Skolnick*   168

Otherwise   *Carol Tokar Pavliska*   171

You Just Had to Be There   *Libby Simon*   174

What a Wonderful World   *Kathleen Hilliard Coyne*   177

VII
RITES OF PASSAGE

Christmas Magic   *Geraldine (Gerry) Trickle*   183

Her Majesty's Muscle   *Beth Schorr Jaffe*   188

The Time-Tailored Table   *Cindy Kauffman*   191

The Loft Bed   *Molly Meyers*   194

Liberty's Timeless Glory   *Renie Szilak Burghardt*   198

Moopy and the Ranger   *Felice R. Prager*   202

Autumn Leaves   *Lynne Layton Zielinski*   205

These Boots Were Made for Walkin'   *Amy Lynne Johnson*   209

VIII
A PARADIGM SHIFT

My Life   *Luci N. Fuller*   215

Democrat Cake   *Tammy Wilson*   220

Martha Stewart in Disguise   *Lillian Quaschnick*   223

Coming Full Circle with Mickey   *Jennifer Gordon Gray*   227

A Bottle of Bubbles   *Mary Sass*   231

The Gift of Validation   *Jennifer Brown Banks*   234

True Rewards   *Diane Gonzales Bertrand*   236

Under the Stars   *Claudia McCormick*   239

IX
HOLY ENCOUNTERS

Discovering Freedom   *Lea C. Tartanian*   245

My Special Angel   *Mary M. Alward*   249

Amazing Gracie   *Jayne Garrett*   254

Lessons from a Box of Toys   *Linda Aspenson-Bergstrom*   258

High-Altitude Believing   *Dena McClung*   261

The Emissary   *Lisa Robertson*   265

Snow Angel   *Elizabeth Krenik*   268

X
ON THE LIGHTER SIDE

The Mannequin   *Edna Miner Larson*   273

Mom's Makeover   *Pamela Jenkins*   275

A Shopping Spree   *Amy Munnell*   277

Technology for the Millennium   *Leigh Senter*   281

Sweepstakes Dreaming   *Lillian Quaschnick*   283

The Hunt for Wild Asparagus   *Jean Schneider*   286

Hawaii Unplugged   *Sheila S. Hudson*   290

More Chocolate Stories?   293

Contributors   295

INTRODUCTION

What do you dream?

At the beginning of a new year, we are all likely to remember our most cherished dreams—or discover new ones. Will they come true this year? Can they come true at all? Is there something we should be doing to help them along? Our dreams beguile us, drive us, and sometimes frighten us. But one thing is certain: they shape our lives.

Chocolate for a Woman's Dreams celebrates this sacred power in seventy-seven true, heartwarming stories by women with many different kinds of dreams. Whether they are seeking to live happily ever after, live fuller family lives, find a spiritual path, or make a rite of passage, they tell deeply personal stories. With them, you will rediscover joy, laughter, and hope. Your desires will be awakened as you discover new ways to fulfill them.

We may be wired for optimism when it comes to our dreams and what we can create in our own lives, but maintaining that optimism can be difficult in the face of the daily grind. The busyness of real life and the routines of each day can wear us down. We need the support of family and friends, and stories like the seventy-seven included here to remind us of our glorious possibilities.

In my own life, I am part of a sacred circle of women. Our purpose is to assist each other in fulfilling our dreams, celebrating our accomplishments, and finding the good in all that happens. We aren't just close friends, we believe for each other when one of us is down. If my confidence wanes, the others remind me of who I really am. When we all need a good laugh, we do something silly together. If one of us is ill or has an important event, the other three each lights a candle, knowing that, through intention, all of our desires will be realized.

With that same intention in your heart, find a cozy place to be with a friend or in peaceful solitude and savor these pages as you dream along with the powerful women who have created this sacred space for you. They know in their hearts that your dreams are about to bloom. May you learn through these stories how to feed and water those wishes you hold most dear. And may you have only sweet dreams!

I
DREAM
WEAVERS

Dreams come a size too big so that
we can grow into them.

JOSIE BISSET

MY WEDDING-DAY
SURPRISE

*T*he *week before the biggest day in my life, my* wedding, I received the news my favorite aunt had been taken to the hospital, and it didn't look like she would make it out for the wedding. I was devastated and worried for her health and disappointed that after all her help in planning the wedding, she would be unable to attend.

The morning of the wedding dawned bright and although I was caught up in the joy and busyness of the day, I felt my Aunt Evelyn's absence at unexpected moments. After the wedding, while having our pictures taken in a nearby park, I nearly asked my sister Kelly to find Aunt Evelyn before I remembered she wasn't there.

After the pictures the wedding party piled into cars to head for our reception. Don's brother Doug, who was best man, shooed Don and me into the backseat and held the front passenger door for Kelly, my maid of honor. Doug slid into the driver's seat and started the car. Don turned to me and holding my hand said, "I have a surprise for you." Doug and Kelly exchanged knowing looks. Everyone seemed to be in on the plan but me. Kelly gave Doug directions as I desperately tried to figure out where we were going. We traveled in the opposite direction we should have taken to get to the reception. Puzzled, I searched for familiar landmarks, and as we turned onto Carling Avenue I realized we were moments from the hospital.

As we pulled up Doug let Kelly, Don, and me out in all our wedding finery; I was still wearing my veil and holding my bouquet of yellow roses and white orchids. As we strode one by one through the hospital's revolving glass doors the muted conversations in the lobby ceased. A woman with a shock of white hair and a worry-furrowed brow gave us a smile. Some stared outright while others gave sideways, surprised glances.

A pang washed over me on the elevator when we came to a stop at Aunt Evelyn's floor. I wanted to take her with us to the reception when we left. As we rustled down the hall in our wedding garb, we encountered more of the same reactions we'd met in the lobby—ooohs and aaahs from the nurses' station, smiles and curious faces peering from behind doors left ajar, people stepping out into the hall to take a better look or to offer congratulations.

On the whole the mood in our wake became festive, so it was no surprise when we entered Aunt Evelyn's room and saw the effect we had on her. She sat in a chair by the window, in her hospital garb, looking out over the blues and greens of the day. When she turned to see me in my wedding dress, her jaw dropped. It seemed like forever before she could get out of her chair and hug me.

We had a long embrace, and she remained silent for a while taking in the spectacle. After a time she said, "I just spoke with your cousin. He said the wedding service was beautiful." She paused, then broke into the biggest grin. "But it couldn't be prettier than this!"

JENNIFER DOBRENSKI

TIPS FOR
SWEETER DREAMING

1. Banish self-doubt! Yes, it's hard to do but with practice you *can* learn.
2. Volunteer your time; helping others will feed your soul.
3. Create a special corner in your home that's yours with an altar displaying your favorite things—a place where you will find peace of mind.
4. Treat yourself at least once a month in your favorite way— manicure, massage, movie, dinner out.
5. Eat a little chocolate! It won't solve your problems but it will make you feel better.
6. Speak your truth with love, and you will be heard.
7. Be the role model you want your children to have.
8. Every day have at least one good belly laugh. It will even help chase away disease!
9. Know that you are here by Divine purpose and discover what that purpose is.
10. If you are single and seeking a mate, continue to live your life fully. You'll be the magnet your perfect partner will be drawn to.
11. When you are unsure of your abilities, *act as if* you *are* sure and you will learn to *feel* sure.
12. Giving your children solid roots now will allow them to blossom later.

13. Share your dreams only with those who will support you unconditionally.
14. Look through your check register to see how you have been spending money. You may want to change your priorities.
15. When you spot flaws in others, chances are you have the same shortcomings.
16. Taking responsibility for everything you do builds your self-esteem.
17. If you are married, praise your partner each day for one of his qualities. It will bring more love into the relationship.
18. Stress is toxic to your well-being. Discover ways to reduce the anxiety in your life.
19. A part of you always *knows* what's best for you. Trust that part.
20. The older you get to be, the more valuable your friends and family become.
21. You'll find the most contentment when talking with God.
22. Remember that you are here to love, laugh, heal the world, and eat chocolate!

KAY ALLENBAUGH

Expect to have hope rekindled.
Expect your prayers to be answered in wondrous ways.
The dry seasons in life do not last.
The spring rains will come again.
SARAH BAN BREATHNACH

MAGIC HAPPENS

Sometimes in the thick of a story, just when you think nothing can possibly save the heroine or hero from a complicated or life-threatening predicament, something magical happens. This occurs so frequently there is a literary term describing the intervention: "deus ex machina," meaning, "a god from a machine." This dramatic device originated in ancient Greek dramas when the plot would become so involved that no other solution seemed feasible. A god would then conveniently appear, often in a basket lowered onto the stage by a crane, to unravel the mess and restore order.

In the last days of my marriage, when I was so depressed I read nothing but children's books and fantasy, I didn't know about that. But I noticed in practically every single story I read that this character would appear just as the weary hero was ready to give up. Sometimes he or she would be magical and give the hero a mysterious amulet. But most often the character was just an ordinary person and simply provided a hot meal or a safe place to stay the night. Filled with renewed strength, the hero could then continue his or her quest.

When I first fled my husband and left all I loved and knew in Missouri, I thought angels and magic amulets and kindly souls were the stuff of children's books. Because if such beings existed *really*, how come none had showed up in my own story? How come they hadn't provided me with a hot meal and comfort after my husband kept me up all night berating me for sins that existed only in his imagination? How come they hadn't given me a safe place to be when he was at his most hateful and violent? And hey, *where was my amulet?*

That was the state of my heart the winter I came out west. I had never been to Oregon before—just picked it out from a map—but it seemed as good a place to live as any. Ocean and mountains and not many people—a promising place to begin a new life. But I hadn't counted on rain every single day and so much fog that half the time I had to navigate by streetlights because I couldn't see to the end of a block. And I hadn't known I'd be so lonely. I now understood why dogs howled at the moon. I had three friends left in the world and they were all in Missouri. My dog, Beau Beagle, was all I knew here. Why had I ever left?

My days fell into a depressing sameness. I'd awaken early to check the few help-wanted ads and make calls or send out résumés, as the ad requested. Then I'd make the employment office rounds. As the weeks wore on I showed up for interviews with increasingly fewer hopes. Times were hard and unemployment was high in Oregon that winter of 1979. Afternoons, Beau and I wound our way through the foggy and rainy coastal range for the ocean. We'd walk the lonely beaches and I'd cry until I felt empty.

Nights, my ex-husband would call to tell me how much he missed me. If only I'd come home, things would be different, Jim promised. I wanted to believe him, but our conversations would almost always end with, "Whatever possessed you to move to a place where you don't know anybody? That's stupid for even you.

You'll never find a job. Who'd hire you?" Still, during those dark and endless nights I missed him and longed for home where everything was familiar.

Weeks passed and I still hadn't found work. I had enough money for about another month's rent and then I had no idea what I was going to do. Maybe Jim was right. Maybe I should just go home. Maybe I was too stupid to live on my own. Maybe things would be different this time as he promised. Maybe.

That afternoon the coast was even colder and foggier than usual. Deserted, it was curiously quiet other than the constant drumming of the ocean. Beau stayed close by my side instead of running ahead as he usually did. Then an old man seemed to appear out of nowhere and with a kind smile on his weathered face asked if I had seen any jasper on the beach. Angrily I snapped, "I wouldn't know a 'jasper' if it were sitting next to me on the bus." *Jerk*, I thought, starting to move away from him. Still, it seemed odd that Beau wasn't barking. Usually he growled deep in his throat if a man even walked past us. Instead, he was sitting calmly in front of the old man, looking intently into his face. Following Beau's lead, I stood still too.

"Well, here. Let me show you." The old man reached into his pocket and pulled out a handful of polished stones. He was retired, he explained, and polished the rocks he found on the beach. He pointed out yellow and green and red jaspers, agates clear and golden or darkly cloudy. Some of the agates had mossy-looking images deep within. Then he offered his jewel-filled hand to me and said, "Here. Pick any three you want. For you are still a child and are far from your home."

I reached into his large, square callused hand and chose a red jasper, a dark-veined jasper, and a golden agate. I closed my eyes and pressed my fingers tightly around the stones' polished smoothness. *Amulets!*

Without another word the old man walked back into the mist. Beau and I stood there for some moments watching him. I didn't wonder where he had come from or how he had known I was far from home. I just knew magic had found me. I put the stones in my pocket and felt peaceful and strong.

I knew coming to Oregon was right. And I knew I could survive. I still had years of healing and struggle ahead of me, but I felt excited and hopeful about my journey. I found a job the next week and made two friends. My new life had started.

And that night I didn't answer my phone when Jim called. I just let it ring and ring.

MARY ZELINKA

I decided to give up the past in order to live my future.
GLORIA ATTAR

I DREAMED OF ITALY

At the tender age of ten, I saw the movie *Three Coins in the Fountain* and it touched me deeply. Someday, I decided, I would live in Italy. Never mind that we lived in Ohio. Never mind that my parents scoffed at my big dream.

Many years later, my beloved husband died suddenly. Pregnant at the time, I was left stranded by his death in our tiny and forever sand-blown apartment in the desert of Utah. With little money, I had no idea of how I was going to manage as a widow and new mother. I remember thinking about Italy at times when I was hurting the most, yet I knew living there would, once again, remain a fantasy. Accepting this reality added pain to my already wounded heart.

I moved back to Ohio feeling my fate was sealed. My parents had purchased a tiny house for me that I hadn't seen, and Mom had already picked out and hung the curtains. Although grateful, I felt like a child again, forever destined to live a life with dreams unfulfilled. I ached and lamented to my best friend that I felt stuck. Having known me for eighteen years, she said, "Gloria, I don't think you'll ever be stuck anywhere. Your address is the only one in my book that I keep in pencil." She was right, but with no idea of how I was going to be the breadwinner and mother and father to my daughter, the future looked bleak.

When my daughter was born, I was afraid to love her too much, fearing she would be taken away from me as well by another catastrophe. I was detached while I took care of her basic needs and gave her the love I felt I could. Looking back, I realize that I was just going through the motions and still numb from my husband's death.

My mother stepped in and began to mother my daughter as she had me, instilling fear of risk taking, stifling my daughter's creativity and independence. I know that she was just doing the best she could, but when I heard her using the same words with my daughter that she had used with me as a child, I started to wake up.

Almost two years had passed, and I was tired of feeling anesthetized by grief. My parents had told me to settle down, buy a house, and stay in one place to build a nest egg. Good advice to be sure, but I didn't feel at home there. I wasn't living, merely existing. I wanted my passion back. My daughter was destined to grow up with a mom who sacrificed everything to give her daughter security, but never lived life. She would more likely believe in herself and her dreams if I provided her with the example and lived mine. I had to choose between keeping the security I had and feeling dead inside, or risking everything to come to Italy. That's when I dusted off my Italian dream and told myself it would be the last winter in Ohio for us.

Over the Internet, I made a contact in Bologna, Italy, with a professor about a teaching job, and he offered me a job teaching English! This was the first sign that, perhaps, my dream might become a reality. As I struggled, and even hesitated at times, with the logistics of relocating, he encouraged me by saying, "You can either dream of living here for the rest of your life, or you can move here. Make the choice." Often I wanted to say back, "But it's not that simple." Yet, in reality, it was.

I called an auctioneer and set a date for the auction of my

house, car, and furnishings. I held a garage sale. I watched as people carried off my antiques (mostly from Italy). My heart fell each time the buyers selected a piece and offered me a nominal amount for it. I steeled myself against crying by imagining the hills of Italy and throwing my coins into the Trevi Fountain. I sold every piece of jewelry I owned. I burned years of journals that had kept pain alive for me. I decided to give up the past in order to live my future. I remember reading something to the effect that you measure a dream by what you are forced to give up in order to attain it. Each time I was faced with selling an item, I reminded myself that I was getting closer to a dream that had been twenty-eight years in the making.

I have lived in Italy for six months and each day I wake up happy. The hills of Bologna are my everyday view with the sanctuary of San Luca looking down on my sleepy little town of Casalecchio di Reno. My heart is settled as I have found my home.

Although the teaching job with the professor didn't pan out, I do teach for another school and have private students. Money is tight, but I feel rich. I now enjoy a closer relationship with my daughter, a priceless benefit. Every day I watch her blossoming into an independent bilingual child. Many times she learns Italian words before I do, and she teaches them to me.

I knew I had—in her heart—become her mother when after two months of living here my two-and-a-half-year-old daughter rolled over before going to sleep and whispered, "Goodnight, Mommy, I love you," and kissed me. She had never uttered these words to me before. I couldn't believe what I'd heard and asked her to repeat it. She said it again, and has, every night since then—sometimes in English and sometimes in Italian.

GLORIA ATTAR

If you look at what you have in life,
you'll always have more.
If you look at what you don't have in life,
you'll never have enough.
OPRAH WINFREY

WARM HANDS, WARM HEART

I've always known my husband was a good man. He's one of those people that everyone loves—men and women alike. Children are drawn to him. Animals adore him.

Years of hard work have left his hands rough and scarred. Yet his touch has always been gentle.

When we brought our firstborn home from the hospital, I looked down into that tiny face peering out of the blankets and was overwhelmed at the awesome gift we had been given—and the profound responsibility. I feared my own inexperience. Each new task was a test, one I feared I would not pass. Mark was always calm. When it was time for our son's first bath, Mark filled the small tub. Gently cradling our son in his left arm, he bathed him with his right hand. When our son was restless and fussy, lying on Dad's chest comforted him. Together, Mark told me, we can do anything. I believe him.

I once caught my husband giving flowers to another woman. She was a pretty blonde who approached him in the store as he picked out flowers for me. She was delighted with the blue-tipped carnation he gave her. Her mother was horrified at her toddler's boldness and offered profuse apologies. "I had to give her a flower," my husband told me. "She has the same name as you."

I've truly been blessed, but in the busyness of everyday life, I sometimes forget to voice my gratitude.

One Sunday morning, we arrived early for services at the church where my husband Mark serves as groundskeeper. Following the tree-lined path to the building, a sharp whistle from one of the small dogwoods bordering the sidewalk startled me.

Mark whistled back. The tree burst into song. Mark replied with a tune of his own. We continued walking and the mockingbird that had been hiding amid the dogwood's leaves darted ahead of us to the next tree. Mark whistled again. Again, he was answered with song.

"Friend of yours?" I asked.

"That's my buddy," he answered.

"So how did you two meet?"

"You know I'm always the first one here in the mornings," he began.

I knew. Mark prided himself on having the doors open, the lights on, and the coffee brewing before everyone else arrived. No one walked into an uninviting office when Mark was on the job.

"Remember the late frost we had a few weeks ago?" he continued. "I found that little fellow on the sidewalk near the door. He was either too young to be afraid, or too cold to care, because he let me pick him up. I warmed him in my hands for about ten minutes until he decided he was thawed out enough and he flew away. Now he sings to me every morning, and he keeps me company in the afternoons when I mow."

Mark whistled one more time as he opened the door. His friend whistled back and flew away.

Inside, on my knees, I looked at the man next to me. His hands, scarred by years of hard work, were folded in prayer. I saw those hands cradled around a shivering bird. I saw again those hands caress the cheek of our son as I nursed him so many years ago. I know well those rough hands—and their warm, gentle touch.

I said thank you.

TAYLOR JOSEPH

LUCY'S LEGACY

I was new to Dallas, Texas, far from my childhood home and family in Wisconsin. By day I worked as an activity director in a nursing home. By night, I was a lonely woman in a strange city where friendships weren't formed easily.

I soon found myself at the local humane society, and it took only a minute to find what I was looking for. She was a small-sized dog covered in long, fluffy white fur. I was sure this ball of fluff was for me. She had other ideas. I was totally ignored by the small white dog, all the while being pestered by a shaggy, scraggly little black thing.

"How long has this critter been here?" I asked.

"Over two months," the woman who was helping me replied. "She will have to be put down tonight to make space for more adoptable dogs."

My heart went out to the black puppy licking my face. Maybe it was her affectionate personality, or the way she danced in circles on her hind legs, or the "take me home" look in her big black eyes. Maybe it was my lonely spirit needing to give her life instead of death. I didn't know; I didn't give it any thought. I just adopted her and drove home.

Once there, she looked right at home. She sat on the rug by the back door as if it had been put there for her exclusive use.

I called the little black dog Lucy and bathed the dirt out of her matted fur. I brushed and clipped until the knots came out.

What had been a shaggy, unkempt pooch at the pound now had shiny fluff and curls for a coat. She ran circles around me as I laughed and thanked God for my new friend.

I got approval from the nursing home administrator to bring Lucy to work. She was a lively pup, but warm and affectionate as well. She started on a test run for two weeks to see how she would do with the patients, but from her first day at the home she fit in perfectly. Those two weeks turned into two years.

Lucy and I would make my morning rounds visiting residents. She brought life into the home and friendship to those who lived there. Many times she'd take off on her own, and I'd always find her on someone's lap, listening to whatever that person had to share. Other times, she'd be curled up at the foot of someone's bed. She offered comfort to everyone who was willing to have a bit of her company. She offered friendship to those who were lonely and love to all who would accept it. As for those who didn't accept it on the spot, she waited patiently, winning them over in the end.

One male stroke victim named Lloyd spent his days sitting in his wheelchair staring into the air. He hadn't spoken since the stroke, had shown no interest in life around him, and needed help to be fed.

I had noticed early on during Lucy's days at the home that she had taken a special interest in Lloyd. Lucy would walk around his chair three or four times before politely depositing her black behind at his feet. It never seemed as though he noticed. I simply let Lucy do her thing.

As the weeks went by, Lucy seemed to prolong her visits to Lloyd a little more each day. What started out to be a ten-minute nap at his feet, turned into a twenty-, then thirty-minute nap. Finally, when a nurse let me know she'd been with him for almost two hours, I decided to check in on them.

Lucy was not on the floor, but in his lap. Lloyd was staring into the air, but one hand gently stroked Lucy's back. In the days to follow, Lloyd was more willing to feed himself. One day, I stopped by to say hello to Lloyd, and he simply closed his eyes. I set a grooming brush on his nightstand and, without a word, left his room.

Two days later, a nurse peeked into his room and saw him brushing Lucy's black, curly fur. We were amazed, but even more so when Lloyd began to brush his own hair.

Next I tried again to convince Lloyd to join an activity. I promised him Lucy would sit with him. I was answered with a bold and icy stare. *This is better than not looking at me at all,* I thought.

One day, about six weeks after Lucy and Lloyd had become friends, Lucy suddenly stopped going into his room. Instead she sat very quietly outside his door. By this time the pair was the talk of the home, and staff and residents alike were bewildered at the dog's new behavior.

But the next day Lucy plopped herself at his door and Lloyd wheeled his own chair to join her at the door. She took her place on his lap and he brushed her coat. He had never even attempted to move the wheelchair on his own—before he met Lucy.

His family was called and given a progress report. They came to visit, and he stared at them, instead of the air, but still had no expression and said nothing.

The doctor wasn't impressed, saying that was as far as Lloyd's progress would ever go.

Lucy had her own prognosis.

Within a month, Lucy and her man friend could be found sitting in the recreation room together. A man and "his" dog. Lloyd still didn't talk, but he now made eye contact with others around him.

For a year, Lucy and Lloyd continued to be close friends. He was her first visit of the day, and her last in the evening. And of course, many other times throughout the day, Lloyd would brush Lucy and feed her tidbits saved from lunch.

On one hot summer day, I had scheduled an appointment immediately after work, one where a dog would not be welcomed. Instead of taking Lucy to work with me, I left her home where it was cool.

I made my morning visits as usual. The conversations were mostly questions as to where Lucy was. When I entered Lloyd's room, and he had not yet seen Lucy, I was met with a scowl and a grunt. I was surprised, not at his anger, but that he had made a sound. It was something no one at the home had heard from him, ever.

Later that day, I stood at the nurses' station and could feel his eyes piercing my back. I suddenly felt a hard object hit me squarely in the back of the head. I turned to find Lloyd directly in back of me and the dog brush on the floor. He'd thrown it at me, and his aim was perfect.

"Where the heck is my dog Blackie?"

I almost jumped directly out of my shoes.

"Are you looking for Lucy?" I asked.

"That's a stupid name. Where is my dog Blackie?"

The man who had rarely looked at anyone, and had not spoken since before his stroke, was talking. There was no speech therapist, no special medicine, no special doctors—only special attention from a little black dog. Six months later, Lloyd was walking, talking, socializing, and finally, going home.

His family had arranged for a home care nurse to visit and take care of the needs he could not. The nursing home staff had taken care of another special need.

As we gathered to wish him well, we gave him a large wiggly box decorated with a huge yellow bow. Lloyd opened the box and a wide grin covered his face as a small black pup jumped out and barked a greeting.

Lloyd scooped the little dog up immediately.
He couldn't, after all, go home without his best friend.

LINDA ASPENSON-BERGSTROM

PAINTED LADIES RULE

I opened our bathroom medicine chest the other day and was blinded by a rainbow. It wasn't caused by the mirror reflecting the sunlight off my fillings. Nor was its source a set of face paints used on Halloween and when I'm having a bad hair day and need a disguise. The rainbow consisted of about a dozen sexy bottles of nail polish that I've accumulated during the past ten months.

In order to understand the significance of this vision, a little background is in order. My medicine chest formerly contained just what everyone else's does: expired antibiotics; petrified syrup of ipecac; and five different kinds of headache remedies, some of which also reduce fever, alleviate inflammation, or simulate the sensation felt by a headless horseman after the wound heals. The only bottle of nail polish found anywhere in our house was a clear substance for stopping runs in my panty hose.

Nail polish was for girls. It seemed like an awful waste of time and money. I preferred to think of my nails as God-given tools. Once I assembled a kid's bicycle with nothing but a paper bag (to swear into) and my fingernails. Why would I consider coating them with lacquer that might interfere with their usefulness?

But then something happened . . . slowly . . . insidiously: I started getting old. Along with all the usual side effects of aging came brittle nails. I went out and purchased brush-on nail strengthener and increased my calcium intake. Now my nails were shiny and strong. I felt important, like a movie star. Or a woman whose children unload the dishwasher.

On Father's Day last year, I redeemed a gift certificate that my husband had given me on Mother's Day. It was for a manicure and pedicure at the local Feet, Fingers, and Face spa. The young manicurist directed me to a rack on the wall where I was to select my color. I started getting dizzy—where was the clear? Why would I want color on my nails? Then I realized how disappointed my husband and sons would be if I came home looking exactly as I had before my spa experience, so I reluctantly picked a subtle shade of mauve and sat down across from the manicurist.

I watched carefully while she set up her tools and towels, and made mental notes as we went along, feeling certain I could do this more cheaply at home the next time. The first step was paying or you risk ruining your manicure by digging out your money. *What a great job,* I thought, *you get paid before doing any work!* The rest of the steps followed with a certain logic: file, soak, apply cuticle remover, push back and clip cuticles, apply clear base coat and two coats of color and clear top coat. Let dry. Drive home without touching the car keys or steering wheel. Tell your family you can't cook or do laundry or take out the garbage for at least twelve hours so your nails can "cure." (I suggest milking your drying time for all it's worth.)

One evening, a few weeks after my spa experience, I discovered that a discount cosmetics shop had opened three doors down from the supermarket. Curiosity, and naked nails, got the better of me. My initial investment in tools and polish paraphernalia set me back about forty bucks, but I'm worth it, right? For dinner that night, we had peanut butter and Tawny Taupe sandwiches.

If you are not ambidextrous, polishing your nails is a lot harder than it sounds. Since I'm a "rightie," my right hand always looks a little worse. Luckily (sadly?), not many people notice because my life is short on handsome strangers who greet me with a kiss on the right hand—or any hand. They seem to prefer my left elbow.

The main reason for the proliferation of polish in my bathroom is that my color preference changes after using a new bottle only once. (I'm a little like this with sandals, too.) And I don't dare try to match my nails with a particular outfit—which is reserved for supermodels and drag queens.

Every couple of months, I splurge on a professional manicure. By then, my cuticles have crept up halfway to my nail tip. This syndrome is best attacked by a two-handed technician with an exotic accent.

My childhood friend Anita, also known as the Empress of Bargain Hunters, was visiting recently from California. Half asleep from her red-eye flight, she dragged me to the mall and headed straight for the high-priced cosmetics counter to check out the special "gift" being offered with a minimum $30 purchase. She sifted through the small bag of giveaways, decided that most of them were worth a try—except the nail polish—and pulled out her checkbook.

Whoever said, "Fate doesn't know from cosmetics," was clearly mistaken because thanks to the Empress, our medicine cabinet has added a new shade of very expensive polish to its ranks: Lancôme's Beige Marilyn.

My shelf life is complete.

MARILYN D. DAVIS

THIS NAME'S FOR YOU

Here in the South of these United States, naming new babies often involves lots of climbing around in family trees. Take, for example, the progeny of Gerald, my husband, and Beth (that's me), also known as Bebe, both as Southern as corn bread and turnip greens. Our eldest is named for her paternal grandfather and both grandmothers; number-two daughter is named for me and my sister; number-one son is named for his maternal grandfather and his father; the lap baby—our end-of-the-line son—is named for his two uncles and his father. Did I leave anybody out?

We're also able to cover a lot of familial territory with our affinity for double names here in Mississippi and parts close by. Names like Will Tom and James Edward and Mary Edith and Lucy Love are commonly shortened to nicknames like "Rabbit" and "Cracker" and "Pumpkin" and "Pookie." But if the need arises, we are not averse to stacking them even higher—Jefferson Davis Poindexter Bumpus III is one that comes (ponderously) to mind. Let's face it, Southerners memorialize their dead—or dying, for we're all heading that direction, of course. My call of bestowal came two years ago.

"Bebe, Bethany went to the doctor this morning and had a sonogram" (this was my wonderful son-in-law Charles calling).

"All right!" I said. "Girl or boy?"

"Another boy."

"Oh, that's great. Wayne needs a brother. They'll have so much fun together."

"We're naming her for you."

"And you've got plenty of hand-me-down clothes, and . . ."

"Bebe, did you hear me? We're naming *her* for you. It's a girl."

"What?"

"I was kidding when I told you it's a boy. It's definitely a girl, and Bethany and I have discussed it. We're naming her for you—your full name. Given name. Maiden name. The whole works."

Can a heart burst with happiness? Does pride know boundaries? My devoted children were giving me the gift of renewed life in the soul of this child yet unborn. The honor was staggering.

When I placed the phone back in its base, I flopped to the floor. Leaning against the bed, I sat with my eyes closed, trying to imagine what the years would bring for this little Beth. Would she play the piano like her Bebe? Would she string words like trinkets, as I so love to do? More than likely not. She'd probably be the athlete I always wished I could be, or the cook I'm not, or the president of the United States . . . or any and all of the above. Check. Check. Check. One thing for certain, she'll have my name, but she'll build her own list of achievements, which is exactly as it should be.

Well, the big birthday came. Charles, his mother, my husband, and I were there in the hospital room when the baby came into this world—a precious, healthy, bellowing miracle. Tears spilled down my cheeks. Was this beautiful cherub truly to be my namesake? We hadn't discussed the name in several weeks. Had Bethany and Charles changed their minds? All fears were then eliminated as Charles picked up the phone and called his dad, Wayne, who was watching the baby's big brother, also named Wayne. My heart races still when I remember that moment.

"Dad," Charles almost shouted, "Beth's here!"

Susan, the paternal grandmother, was as thrilled with the baby's name as I was. Her oldest child, a daughter, has her name and plans to pass it down to a daughter.

Isn't it confusing having people in the family with the same names? Not at all. Once you're a grandfather or grandmother you acquire a new name—Granddaddy, or Pop, or Gran, or Nana or something else equally charming. I'm Bebe now.

The only problem this *nom d' honeur* has caused in my life is the elevation of my meddling inclinations. When I see a young couple about to be parents, I want badly to pull them aside and whisper, "Y'all listen to me. Name that baby for your mamas!" I wish I could tell these young folks that all the popular, fad names in the book could never give their child the sense of precious heritage that only a beloved family name can. And I'd tell them that for a grandparent, an aunt, an uncle, or a special friend, there's no more splendid laurel than to have a namesake.

Beth Boswell Dowdy is a wonderful little person. Every time I look at her, I swell with pride. Is there not some yearning in each of our hearts for one small tangible sign of immortality? All of Beth's life, you see, when I'm long gone and forgotten by almost everybody else, she'll tell folks, "I was named for my maternal grandmother." And there will probably be many more Beth's in our family in the generations to come. There's something as comforting about that as my Aunt Elizabeth's threadbare quilt on the foot of my bed.

BETH BOSWELL JACKS

II
HAPPILY EVER AFTER

Happiness is not a station you arrive at,
but a manner of traveling.

MARGARET LEE RUNBECK

I MARRIED A
MILLIONAIRE

*If I won a million dollars, I would give it to someone
who needs it more than I do.* For you see, while this may
come as a surprise to our employers and to the nice folks at
the Wells Fargo Bank, who take such things as deposits and our
pesky end-of-month balance very seriously, I am married to a millionaire.

Allow me to explain.

Spotting my husband in a crowded airport terminal makes
me light up with pleasure. At times I have glimpsed the goofy
grin plastered on my face and decided, upon reflection, that
a goofy grin of this magnitude is worth several hundred dollars.

My husband arrived by police car for the birth of our child.
After the truck had towed away the remains of the car he'd totaled while rushing to the hospital, he was left stranded on the
side of the road, and a helpful police officer delivered him to
the doorstep in time to help me with my breathing exercises.
The cost of one crumpled Toyota? A few thousand dollars. But
it was priceless being present the first time the new father held
his son.

Laughter is the best medicine, so it goes, and the mental images
of my millionaire husband playing hide-and-seek with an Irish set-
ter, or giving the cat a bath in the sink, or helping our child with a
class assignment that involved constructing a Spanish mission

from sugar cubes always makes me laugh. I'm positive those memories spare me a costly trip to the pharmacy.

What do millionaires do for fun on quiet evenings at home? We dance. Waltz, polka, fox trot—our repertoire is large—and the fact that we don't actually know the steps doesn't prevent us from enjoying ourselves. The savings in dance lessons are considerable. Sometimes we just put on some good belly-rubbing music—the kind that doesn't require fancy footwork. I'm rich when I'm dancing in the arms of my millionaire husband.

I've seen this man bow at the bedside of our sick child, knowing his prayers must surely match my urgent pleas that were storming heaven, and I've seen his face flood with relief when the doctor arrived to say the tests were normal.

My father never approved of the young men I dated. In my nightmares I was a spinster in my sixties and my father, strict and stern, was still managing to scare off would-be suitors. Now that I'm a parent myself, I understand that, in his eyes, no one came up to the standards he'd set for his only daughter. I'll never forget linking my lace-draped arm in his strong one as we walked up the chapel aisle to join my future husband at the altar, or how tightly he held me to his side.

The night my dear father died, my husband held me tightly while I sobbed my way through two pillows, the top sheet, and the bottom sheet before I headed to the guest room in search of a bed with dry linens. I wish I could tell my father that this young man was a keeper. His compassion, my friends, is worth more than jewels.

Over the last twenty-five years, many were the times we had more days in the month after we'd reached the end of our money. But we've always had each other, and our home is filled with love and laughter.

My heart is full of love for my millionaire husband. His devotion and commitment warm and comfort me, and enrich my life.

These are more valuable than all the gold bullion in Fort Knox, and thanks to him I am fabulously wealthy.

LANA ROBERTSON HAYES

CONFESSIONS OF AN
ADDICT

"My name is Betty, and I'm an e-mailaholic."

That's what I'll say when I find a support group. An ugly word "addiction," but I fear that's what it is. This is how it started:

Three months ago, I joined an on-line writing group. This group of aspiring writers encouraged each other to write at least thirty minutes daily to keep up their creative energy. Finding thirty minutes a day to write was not my problem. Finding thirty minutes a day *not* to write was. Imagine what it's like now, three months later . . . much worse. When I became active in my writing group, e-mailing back and forth several times a day with our work and our comments, I stopped going to my daily exercise class.

While my literary skills are improving, my body is losing the tone gained from months of water aerobics. My children don't call me their "jock mother" anymore. I love that name, and I miss it. At my peak I felt as fit as a fiddle. Now after sitting far too long at the computer, my body aches in several places, and my house and yard are in complete disarray.

The time had come to break this cycle of endless reading and writing e-mail, so yesterday I turned over a new leaf. I made a commitment to return to water aerobics. I gathered my equipment and laid my bathing suit by the bed as a reminder that tomorrow I would not go downstairs in my housecoat and open my e-mail, as usual. I always opened my e-mail before my eyes and stayed undressed like that till noon. But tomorrow would be different. I would dress in my bathing suit first thing in the morning and go to the eight o'clock class. With enthusiasm for my journey toward recovery, I set the alarm.

The alarm rang at seven-fifteen the next morning. I shut it off. The sight of my bathing suit on the chair made me ill. How could I have thought I would actually jump out of bed, put on that bathing suit, and drive two miles to get wet? I must have been crazy. I skipped the eight o'clock class, staying in bed to wrestle with my conscience instead.

I finally put on the suit, feeling cold and uncomfortable, and forced myself to drive to the nine-thirty class. Upon my arrival, too many people greeted me, saying they'd missed me and asking where I had been. I didn't dare tell them I had returned to class to put an addiction behind me, start my life over, and get myself back in "jock" mode so I could clean the house and garden. Instead, I said, "I simply got sidetracked [charming laugh], but I'm back for good." I tried hard to believe it.

A new instructor led the class, a strong-voiced, young, tan, athletic chick. The workout was a killer. I faked my way through and felt better for it, but only in my head. I had forgotten my water bottle. My body felt bad. I couldn't see straight. I was terribly out of shape from sitting in one place for three months in front of the computer screen.

This was a good lesson for me, as it would help me see the error of my unhealthy ways. With only one class under my belt, I knew I was on my way to recovery. A great many thoughts ran through my mind between the pool and my car. It was not a long way, but it took a long time because I couldn't walk straight. While driving home, I resolved to change my habit of checking e-mail every hour.

I stumbled into the house as weak as a kitten and too weary to think. I moved in a daze, sat down in the desk chair in my wet bathing suit, and stared at the blank screen. I had barely enough strength to eagerly reach for the mouse and raise my shaky forefinger to click. I stayed there until my bathing suit was dry.

BETTY AUCHARD

When love comes it comes without
effort, like perfect weather.
HELEN YGLESIAS

A WANT-AD BONUS

I read the "roommate wanted" ad again, carefully scru-
tinizing each word. Picking up the telephone I dialed the
accompanying number. I was surprised when a deep mascu-
line voice answered. It had never occurred to me that the other
roommate might be male. After a brief conversation we made an
appointment to meet. I was a graduate student in Boston and des-
perate for a place to live.

My mother was outraged that I would even consider such an
arrangement. I explained to her that many girls in cities live pla-
tonically with boys, but she refused to see my side.

"You don't know this person," she bristled. "He could be anything, some kind of pervert, a sadist, even an ax murderer. I cannot believe you would think of such a thing, much less actually
do it!"

I was not an idiot, I told her. I would have a lock on my door, a
cell phone by my side. I could even get a license to carry mace. No
amount of persuasion on my part would change her mind.

Jeff was delightful. Because he was a physical education teacher
at a private boys' school, he was quite an example of physical fit-
ness himself. He was new to the area. He'd just recently moved to

Boston and had left his family and his longtime girlfriend behind in Connecticut.

I moved in the following week after my mother made an inspection tour of the neighborhood, the apartment, and most pointedly, of Jeff. He was affable and helpful; amused at the close surveillance he was subjected to. I could tell my mother remained unconvinced. She took one final walk through the apartment before departing, probably on the lookout for his ax.

I began classes and was fortunate to find a part-time job in a small clothing boutique. Jeff and I fell into our separate routines and seldom saw each other.

Except on Wednesday nights.

It just so happened that Jeff did not have school commitments on Wednesday evenings, and I didn't work that night either. We spent pleasant hours talking about our families and friends.

Jeff told me about his girlfriend, Heidi, whom I had talked to several times on the phone. She and Jeff had met when they were freshmen at the University of Connecticut. She went on to work for an investment firm in New York City while he had come to Boston to teach. He had gone there a couple of weekends to see her, and she was coming to Boston the following month. Fortunately, she did not think our living arrangements strange. I knew several girls at Northeastern who had male roommates. They definitely felt it was a safety measure.

Time marched on and we continued with our own schedules, still meeting up with each other on Wednesday nights. Sometimes we would share a pizza or take-out Chinese.

One night Jeff said, "I have a favor to ask you."

"Sure," I answered, expecting to be asked to pick up his dry cleaning or a package at the post office.

"My school is having a dinner dance for the faculty next week. Heidi and I have decided not to conduct a long-distance romance and won't be seeing each other anymore. I was wondering if I could bribe you to go with me?"

I was rather surprised at the request and it must have shown in my expression.

"Just as friends," he assured me. "I really need to put in an appearance."

"Okay," I agreed, and we made our plans.

We had a great time at the dance. I met Jeff's school friends and his principal. They were friendly and welcoming. I felt right at home. On the ride home curiosity got the better of me.

"I'm wondering," I said to him. "You must know plenty of girls in town by now. Why did you ask me to go to the dance with you?"

"Well," he began, "I knew the principal's wife would be there as well as all the people I work with. I wanted to show up with someone very presentable. You immediately came to mind."

I could see he was grinning. I was not sure if I should take that explanation as a compliment or not.

"Just what is so presentable about me?" I persisted.

"Your legs." He continued to grin. "You have unforgettable legs. They caught my attention the day you moved in. You remember, the day your mother looked like she wanted to throttle me." That made me giggle.

"I didn't think you noticed."

"It was pretty obvious what she thought from the way she glared at me and bared her teeth." We were both laughing helplessly by the time I finished telling him about the retaliation I had had in store for him had he made any unwelcome moves on me.

After that night there was a definite change in our friendship. I began to find myself thinking about Jeff at work, at school, and in any spare moment I had. Could I be falling for my roommate?

Wednesday nights took on a new meaning. We went out together for quick dinners, sometimes a movie or just a walk around the neighborhood. Suddenly, we were dating.

Our relationship grew more and more serious. We became engaged and my mother changed her tune. Jeff was no longer the villain she had predicted. She quickly made the transition from skeptic to mother of the bride. Today her conversations center on her "wonderful grandchildren, her marvelous son-in-law, and her lucky, lucky daughter."

ALICIA WILDE HARDING

THE SLEEPWALKER

I woke again standing in the middle of the kitchen in a cold sweat. As a child, I had often walked in my sleep when excited about some upcoming event. This was different.

Our third son had been born twenty-four weeks into my third pregnancy. He weighed one pound twelve ounces and had spent his first three months in the neonatal unit. My husband and I had been on an emotional roller-coaster those three months, but thought once we brought Jordan home, life would stabilize. It had somewhat, except at night. Since his move home, I'd begun sleep-walking each night, waking up in a different room of the house. Three weeks after Jordan came home, the lack of sleep began to tell. With Jordan's needs and a two- and four-year-old to wrestle, I worried my exhaustion might lead to impatience, illness, even injury.

Each night as I climbed into bed depleted by yet another day of too much to do and too little sleep, I'd offer gratitude for my family, my community, the hospital staff who'd tended to Jordan those first three months, and drift off relaxed, in a positive frame of mind.

Maybe I'd sleep.

The morning after my husband found me in the basement, he gently approached the subject of my getting some counseling. I couldn't believe he thought I needed professional help, yet I wasn't making any progress on my own. Still, I held out another week, figuring I didn't have the time, or a sitter, to allow me to go to a counselor. Finally, the sleep deprivation tipped me over the edge, and I scheduled an appointment.

At the first session, I detailed the events of the past year and realized I'd undergone a great deal of stress. However, I explained to the counselor that hiring a baby-sitter on a regular basis, especially with Jordan's high needs, was out of the question.

"I need to be home with him," I said.

At that the counselor locked my gaze and said, "Well, we'd better get to work!"

I described to him my recurrent nightmare of something evil chasing me.

"I can't tell you what it is because I'm too afraid to face it. I run and then wake up sweaty and breathless somewhere other than my bed."

He sat back and exhaled. "The only way to beat this then is to turn and face your fear. If it's a dragon or a bear, kill it or put it in a cage. Do whatever it is you need to do to feel safe. What's important is taking charge of your fear. Once you can do this, your nightmares will cease."

I left his office holding this hope and the determination that no matter how scary, I'd confront my fear. That night I fell into a deep sleep and then I began to feel the familiar dread. Every inch of me wanted to jump and run, but I held my ground and turned. Lying on my bed was a tiny baby outfit. The clothing had a 3-D look, as if the baby had just been lifted out. Next to the outfit hovered an angel, all in black.

"Are you the angel of death?" I asked.

He nodded.

"You're not going to take Jordan, are you?"

He shook his head no.

With that I drifted into a deep, peaceful sleep. In the morning, as I shared my dream with my husband, I saw how much my fear made sense. Even though, against all odds, Jordan was healthy and at home, a part of me still feared he might die. But once I confronted my fear, head on, the nightmare stopped and a sense of peace filled that space.

Jordan is eleven years old now, and he loves to hear this story. I love telling it because it reminds me of a time I learned that the only way to conquer my fears is to meet them head on.

ELEANOR McLAUGHLIN

QUEEN OF THE AISLES

A trip to Costco is always more fun than chore. One never knows what tasty giveaways a generous woman will be handing out, or what irresistible gift baskets will be packaged and designed to please any recipient. The best outing ever had to be a result of my friend Marianne's dreadful accident in Africa.

Marianne's taste for adventure runs a bit more to the exotic than my safaris to the mall. She has rafted down the Colorado, sea-kayaked off the coast of Alaska, and taken a train trip from London through Russia to Hong Kong. Marianne might go to Cairo for Christmas break while I might go shopping.

A year ago she left for a ten-day photo journey of Kenya with some worldly friends. While on an outing halfway through the itinerary, she stepped over a deadly snake and slipped on a leaf-covered rock, smashing her ankle and leg bone twelve ways from Sunday. After a night of lighting flares to alert the Flying Doctors, she was transported to Nairobi for surgery. The screws and brackets they used would have been a lot less expensive purchased at you know where. After a difficult flight back home through London, she was housebound, forbidden to drive or work for weeks.

Marianne was restless and bored, and we had to do something about it. Restaurants were awkward, a movie impossible. Strolling along at a spring flower show? Out of the question.

I realized that Costco offered yet another enticement that I had not taken advantage of yet—the red dolly cart. We had no qualms, just confidence that this trip would help to lift her morale.

Marianne had crutches and a serious leg brace, so when we arrived and asked for the big cart, a helpful employee at the West Springfield store didn't blink.

"Why, of course. What a good idea," he said.

We had brought a couple of pillows for Marianne's back. Once we eased her down and got her comfortable, I started steering the cart around the roomy aisles. Cleopatra on a big, red, steel barge. Slowly we picked out things we needed . . . oooh! Good deal on videotapes. That nest of bowls would make a great shower gift. Picture frames. A silk potted ficus. All of these things were placed decorously around Marianne and we wheeled on.

What made the trip even better was the reactions of the adults we passed. Reluctant male shoppers were suddenly smiling and asking their wives if they could get wheeled around. Women came up and congratulated us on our ingenuity—even going so far as to say that shopping never looked like more fun.

Meanwhile, we were stacking steaks and loins of pork around Marianne's knees. We bought books for her to read during her convalescence and big jars of fruit and baba ghanoush and biscotti so meals would be easy. She insisted on paying for a huge bottle of detergent, since I had agreed to do her laundry during the interim. We waved at smiling customers, telling anyone who asked all about the African accident. Somehow it felt as though everyone in the building was enjoying his or her day just a little bit more.

Some communities complain about the lack of personal attention with big chain stores and fight to keep them out of town, but I cannot picture a place that was more accommodating or friendlier than Costco on that Saturday excursion.

A short time later, my husband took a new job. I wound up fifteen hundred miles away from a friendship that's lasted thirty years. I continue to play it safe with an occasional stroll down the aisles of Costco while Marianne continues to feed her travel wanderlust. Next week she flies to Spain and might take a side trip to Turkey. "Life is short," she says, "and there are so many things to see. So what if I get a little banged up along the way." Outings with my friend Marianne remains one of the things I miss most of all.

BEVERLY C. LUCEY

Husband and cat missing . . .
$100 reward for cat.
LINDA GRAYSON

ODE TO JOY

*T*he blue of evening darkens. I recline in a lilac caftan in my cushy oatmeal leather love seat with my Balinese cat Lexie, the color of brandy and cream, asleep on my tummy. Beside me, on a myrtlewood table, steam rises leisurely from the peppermint tea in my favorite blue-and-white ceramic mug. It feels sublime to rest my head on one soft arm of the love seat, while my bare feet dangle across the other, and my fingers dance in air to the rhythms of Beethoven's "Ode to Joy."

This profound contentment, in my seventy-second year, rewards me for a decision I made about a year ago: the decision to take responsibility for my own life. Until then, I had believed my value as a person depended on pleasing some man who would love me and marry me and give me emotional and financial security for the rest of my life.

You'd think, back at my fifty-sixth year, I'd have battered my heart against enough lovers to know the folly of that reasoning. But, no, I was game to try again, and placed a personal ad. Brian responded. We met. He was nice-looking, healthy, solvent, and he opened up his life and gathered me into it. It seemed a comfortable bower of approval, affection, and security, and I snuggled in like a contented kitten in a warm lap.

It's fitting that we spent our brief honeymoon on the Oregon coast, for in this place one can encounter devastating "sneaker waves" that sweep in to engulf you in their frigid waters. So it was in this place and during the first days of our marriage that my husband changed dramatically—and changed everything between us. *Was I imagining things, or would this pass?* I asked myself. For before me now stood the man whose quiet warmth and playful affection I had embraced, if not with the unbridled passion of youth, at least with a trusting kind of love—yet now he was suddenly distant, secretive, and even controlling! I felt as though a huge, cold sneaker wave had washed away the man I'd married and left in his place a great dark stone.

We are both civilized people, Brian and I, so we lived out our fifteen years in a state of civil cooperation. We built a home on the coast. We built a social life. I kept house; he paid bills on time and kept the garden neat. We each pursued our separate interests. Neither of us is a bad person, but neither of us had to give what the other needed, at least, not to each other. Brian seemed fine with that, but I lived in a continual state of conflict with myself. I felt longing and frustration at the total lack of affection and real communication between us. I felt degraded that Brian seemed to regard me, not as a beloved wife, but as a somewhat unsatisfactory employee. I wanted to leave, but felt constrained by my own guilt and fear. Guilt because I had promised to love, honor, and obey till death should part us—and I knew I had failed. Fear because of advancing age and limited financial resources of my own.

At last, after years of listening to my litany of complaints, a friend said, "If it's all that bad for you, why don't you just leave? Don't you have any backbone at all?"

In shock and anger, I left her house and hit the beach where

I pounded the sand with my heels until at last I fell, in tears, against a giant, weathered log. I let myself cry, then made myself think.

"I've tried to love this man," I said to the thundering surf. "But I don't. I can't. Soon, we'll grow old. We'll fall apart. Without love, I can't face it. If I leave, I'll be poor and alone. If I stay . . ." And I pictured the bleak, cold years ahead. I'd been angry with my friend for saying what she had, but her words struck a chord of truth that reverberated in my heart like a great melodic gong.

After all of the agonizing, it seems incredible how smoothly everything went once my decision to be accountable to myself was made. To my relief and delight, the house sold quickly, and I found my financial situation a tad brighter than I had feared. Social Security, investments that had grown over the years, plus a share of the house proceeds would provide a modest, but adequate income. A sense of rightness, for both Brian and me, banished all doubt and all guilt. The spark of my own spirit had grown since the day of my decision, when I'd faced myself on the beach. Now I faced myself again, but this time I smiled, realizing I felt stronger and surer than I ever had before.

My life is simple now, and suits my soul. I read and write at random, listen to classical music during the "news" hour, eat Ramen noodles at midnight, and discuss the ways of the world with friends—some of whom I find on park benches. I just finished my training now, as a volunteer in mental health, and hope to help depressed older women to more positive perspectives, even if they've encountered some sneaker waves. All these things give me a deep sense of personal control and of belongingness in the world, an almost tangible joy.

Sometimes, I'll admit, I wish someone would call when they don't; I think how nice it would be to have a "significant other." Yet, loneliness is not pervasive. Old friendships still prevail and a few new ones are growing. Most important though: I find, after all these years, that my very best friend is myself.

Lexie wakes, stretches, and wanders off to the kitchen for a nibble, and Beethoven's soaring celebration of the spirit begins again. It is his "Ode to Joy." And mine.

PHYLLIS JAMISON

NO PLACE LIKE HOME

Almost five years ago, my husband Keith and I rented a charming little house—a manicured front yard, cozy bedrooms, and a handcrafted oak kitchen lit by morning sun. Then one day our friend Gary, who owned our rental, asked if we'd be interested in purchasing it. Keith and I broke out in huge grins. We relished the thought of becoming homeowners. The only hitch? Gary's asking price was out of our range. Yet having given ownership some thought, we weren't ready to let the idea go. We decided to contact a real estate agent to see what else was on the market.

Our agent gave us a list of homes in our price range that we could go look at alone. Keith and I drove for hours—after work, on weekends—checking each one off our list as we went. None of them ever felt quite right. Either the yard was nonexistent or chock full of weeds, or the yard was perfect but the house needed work. The search began to take on a discouraging tone until we pulled into the driveway of a home that melted my heart.

The house was on a corner lot with lots of trees shading a rich green yard. In the back a swimming pool shimmered, and best of all, this home was walking distance from our rental, so we already knew we liked the neighborhood. We peered through all the windows and loved the inside, too. It couldn't have been more perfect.

We contacted our real estate agent, and he told us the house was vacant due to a last-minute job offer the owner had received. If all went well, we could move right in. Keith and I took a deep breath and made our first ever home offer. That night we walked over to the house and around to the back deck off the pool. The reflection from the night's moon shone into the pool—mesmerizing and peaceful. We sat under the stars pretending the house was ours. We held hands and prayed, each taking turns telling the other our dreams of what we could do to make this house into our home.

Suddenly, I remembered an evening walk several years earlier during the holiday season. We had walked past this very house and admired its proportions, its position on the lot, the plantings, and now here we were potential owners.

While waiting for the loan approval process to be finalized, we fell into the routine of visiting the house each evening after work.

One night, on our way out the door of our rental, Keith stopped.

"Honey, wait here," he said. "I'll be right back!"

The next thing I knew, the car was backing out of the driveway. He reached over and shoved open the passenger door.

"Get in," he said. He had this mischievous, naughty boy look.

After a few minutes we turned into the driveway of the home we'd made the offer on.

"What's going on?" I asked.

He stepped out of the car, opened the trunk, and then scurried over to the "For Sale" sign, which he promptly yanked out of the ground and threw in the trunk! I nearly bent double laughing. I couldn't believe a grown man was worried someone would beat us to the punch, but then again, I probably would have done the same thing myself if I'd thought of it!

Just as we began to back out of the drive, we heard a deep voice hidden in the shadow.

"Are you the new neighbors?"

We grinned, feeling a touch guilty, and said, "We hope so."

A friendly looking man with white hair, glasses, and a round belly stepped toward us.

"Paul," he said and stuck out his hand. I knew, right then, he'd be a terrific neighbor.

A few days later a replacement sign showed up. On our evening walks Keith pulled out the duplicate sign and laid it flat on the lawn so no one driving by could see it.

One night as we sat in our spot under the stars next the to pool and glanced up at the evening sky, a shooting star arched over-head. We knew it was a sign. Later that evening, we received a call that Keith's Grandma Leaver had passed away earlier in the evening.

"That star," Keith said, "it was her watching over us."

The very next morning we received news that the loan had gone through; the home was ours. The first thing we planted was a tree in Grandma Leaver's honor because she was the one so fond of saying, "There's no place like home."

VALENTINA A. BLOOMFIELD

UNDER FOOT

Once she married Jake Yarborough, life was hell on earth for my friend Eila Mae. Heaven knows she'd been warned about how tightfisted he was, but nothing would do her but marry him.

Now any fool knows that just because a fellow has money, it doesn't mean he's going to spend it.

Well, I reckon Eila Mae learned that the hard way. Each time she'd fix to go shopping, Jake would grumble about money, and she didn't necessarily have to go uptown for that to happen, either. Once she bought a new dress mail order, but as soon as it came, Jake had her send it back.

"No use wasting good money on ready-made," he told her. "That's what you got a sewing machine for."

Like a whipped dog, Eila Mae shipped the dress back and kept on buying yard goods and thread even though Jake got himself nice store-bought suits—whenever they went on sale. It was downright lopsided of him being as how he was with his wife, but that's the way he was.

When it came to eats, Eila Mae was expected to keep a garden and buy no more staples than some pioneer woman on the frontier, and that was the truth. Coffee, tea, matches, things you can't grow or make yourself. That's all that came home in her grocery bag.

Now one time when Jake and Eila Mae were driving back from his cousin's funeral up on the Virginia line, they'd stopped to eat at a cafeteria. Jake shoved his tray on past the cashier, not acting like Eila Mae was even with him. Of course he was decked out in his Sunday best, and he was well into his lunch by the time she could even sit down.

She told him, "Jake, I had to pay for my own meal."

So he said, "Well, you're the one who's eating it, ain't you?"

I suppose Eila Mae gave him one of her hang-dog looks and kept quiet like she always did, poor soul.

Now for their whole entire married life, Jake controlled his wife. Why, he'd give her the evil eye when she took a notion to go to the beauty parlor. That was an extravagance he didn't like either. He shelled out the same pittance every week for expenses and so forth, telling her to waste not, want not. Well, she might not have wasted anything, but she sure wanted for plenty.

Once I was at Eila Mae's when she was thinking about repapering the kitchen. Jake put his foot down.

"This paper hung here by my mama long before you moved in here, and I reckon it can last a whole lot longer."

Jake was so ornery he never took sick a day in his life, but once when he was getting up in years, he went out to hunt pheasants in damp weather. Of course these were pheasants Eila Mae would have to clean and dress, mind you.

Well, next thing you know, Jake came down with pneumonia, but he didn't go to the hospital. No, sir! That would have cost too much. As usual, Eila Mae didn't buck him, and within a couple of days, he was deader than four o'clock.

Most of the town turned out for the funeral, wondering if Jake would realize how much it was costing him to die and then come back to life. That would have beat all.

Of course there was an equal amount of speculation about what he'd leave Eila Mae, now that she was a widow woman. Some said he'd take all his money with him since he didn't have a will. Drawing one up was way too expensive. But what Jake hadn't figured on was that the state had one ready for him. With no other living relatives, the man's entire fortune went to Eila Mae and there's no doubt he'd turn over in his grave if he knew what happened next.

First thing she did was go to town and buy herself a fine new pair of pinking shears. Now folks didn't think much about that, being as how handy she was with needle and thread, but when the new curtains appeared at the window and furniture trucks started showing up, they really got to talking. It was clear Eila Mae was like a pup cut loose from a chain without that ornery cuss of a husband around. And I can't say we blamed her much.

It wasn't long until curiosity got the best of Myrtle and me, so we decided we'd have the place a look-see. The Yarborough house was just an old foursquare, nothing fancy, so we tried to imagine what the inside must be like, whether she'd gussied it up like a city house or just what.

Well, we went over with a plate of Myrtle's date bread that Eila Mae was so fond of and sure enough, she invited us in and what a sight to behold! The old things were replaced with a modern couch, a shiny new dining room suite, lamps, and a runner up the front stairway.

"Jake left it so I don't want for anything," Eila Mae said.

That was no lie. The whole place smelled of fresh paint and new furniture—that varnishy smell that makes you think you're in a store.

As we were taking it all in, Myrtle remarked about the braided rug. You never saw such a conglomeration of wool, gabardine, and silk in all your life, and there it lay under foot in the middle of the front room.

"Where did you get that?" Myrtle said.

Eila Mae perked up. "It's custom-made."

"Custom made? Must've cost you right much," I said.

Well, Eila Mae gave us the biggest grin you ever saw. "I did it all by myself," she said. "I didn't have to buy nothing but the scissors."

We knew at that instant what she'd gone and done with those

new pinking shears. I tried to imagine Eila Mae sitting at her sewing machine with a smile of satisfaction as she sewed up strips of Jake's suits, shirts, and ties, making them into that rug.

Yes, sir, she sure beat all.

TAMMY WILSON

III
FAMILY
HIGHLIGHTS

Call it a clan, call it a network, call it a tribe, call it a family.

Whatever you call it, whoever you are,

you need one.

JANE HOWARD

REEL TIME

There was a feeling of pure joy whenever Dad announced he'd be showing our home movies. While waiting for the first huge silver reel, my brothers and I began the ritual of creating shadow bunnies—our fingers diving, colliding, and bending against the stark white wall.

Vintage cartoons preceded the films: they were black and white, starring an anorexic Mickey Mouse. Like the films, the cartoons were silent, but the darkened room where we sat shoulder to shoulder roared with our laughter and commentary. No one "shushed" anyone. There wasn't any dialogue to miss—just the cranking of that old 16mm projector as it echoed through our small split-level home.

For me, an awkward adolescent, the home movies affirmed that I was loved. In the scratchy, faded images I saw my face cupped and kissed by my grandmother, the family matriarch, my loyal best friend. At birthdays Mom and I, hands clasped, led "ring around the rosy" with plump little cousins in party hats. The camera nose-dived when Dad, apparently, ran after me as I tried to maneuver a shaky two-wheeler down a narrow driveway. We poked each other, embarrassed by any shot of our parents' smooching. Dad slim in Navy whites, Mom's Rita Hayworth hair swept in a snood. Had he deliberately set up the camera to record this for prosperity? Hungrily, we absorbed reel after reel, anticipating the flapping sound, our signal to whine for another.

There was the face that seemed to freeze-frame the action, halt our laughter—a favorite aunt who had died suddenly. Years later, I learned she had taken her own life. Watching her braid my hair in these films, I relived the sadness of losing her—the hushed voices at the time of her death.

Then, when I was in high school, Dad began traveling. There was less time for family recreation, and fewer home movies taken. It felt as if we were all being catapulted into the future, and I wondered if there'd ever be another chance to look back and reflect on who we really were as a family.

After I married, my parents and brothers moved to Florida. My husband and I moved to Boston, and for the first time the family was really scattered. When I became pregnant, before buying a single book on prenatal care, I raced to a camera store to purchase a super-8 movie camera and projector. I was fanatical about recording the pregnancy on film, as well as friends' visits, casual dinners, and poker games in our crowded walk-up.

With my camera slung over my shoulder, I was dedicated to my new role as family historian, filming my own children's parties, dance recitals, vacations—starring parrots and dolphins. I edited animated stills at each film's opening, but I was aware of how staged my movies seemed. They were too modern, these "talkies."

For me, they lacked the richness of pure motion and the magical charm reflected in the smoky silences—which were the films of my childhood.

Then one day my father pulled the old reels from storage. He'd seen an ad for transferring them to video, dubbed music included. Not long after, my brothers and I each received a cassette. It was labeled: *Home Movies . . . Our Children*. It had been decades since we watched these movies together, and now we each viewed them separately, 1,500 miles apart, in our own homes with our own families.

The video opens with Paul Anka singing "The Times of Our Lives," and I break down before the first frames. I'm startled by a familiar image of me at three trying to blow out the birthday candles on a fluffy pink cake. My lips curl and quiver until some help appears behind my shoulder. To my surprise the candles go out, and I beam a gummy smile toward the camera. I watch these movies alone wrapped in an old crocheted blanket. My heart pounds and I'm afraid to blink—it's like seeing things for the first time. There's a strange mix of loss and reacquaintance. My grandmother, her hair in a perfect chignon, looks cautious and worried as she walks beside me. The aunt whose death forever haunts me flinches from the camera lens. She is self-conscious and unsure. My parents embrace in a passionate kiss. When did I ever see them kiss like this? I'd forgotten. I find myself talking aloud to the faces, until the video abruptly fades to black, and I sit staring at a blank screen. I call my dad to thank him. "Yes, the video store did a great job." He tells me the cartoons were too old to transfer. "Save them, Daddy," I say.

Another decade passes. My oldest daughter is getting married in forty-eight hours. She announces that following tradition, she will spend the night before the wedding in our home, sleeping in her old bed. She warns she wants a quiet evening, no guests or stress. For hours, I rack my brain over how to spend this special night. And then the idea comes to me, like a forgotten lyric. I call my youngest daughter from the car and ask her to gather the shopping bags containing our super-8 films. We rush to a local camera shop. Yes, they do transfers. Of course, I'll pay double for the overnight service.

After an early dinner, I blindfold the bride-to-be, and her sister guides her to the den, practically pushes her in the rocker. We're all giggling, and she begins to balk, wedding nerves intruding. I turn on the VCR and Paul Anka starts to croon. Removing the blindfold, she sees a four-day-old version of herself—a baby Buddha nuzzled in my arms. I hear her hearty laugh but tears are brimming. Then a small voice says, "Thank you, Mommy."

The gift I give her—these home movies—are the films of *her* childhood, a catalog of *her* young life. If she should ever stray, forget her past, she will have them, as I have mine—some indelible proof of how much she is cherished.

SANDE BORITZ BERGER

BOYS AND WHEELS

M y son was a jittery mass of nerves the morning I took him to the Department of Motor Vehicles for his driving test.

He kept asking, "What if I fail?"

I tried not to notice when the chewing gum fell out of his mouth. It doesn't necessarily follow that if he can't chew gum and talk, that he shouldn't be behind the wheel of an automobile, does it? I steadfastly refused to entertain thoughts such as those, although I'll admit to being thrilled at finding a lucky penny on the asphalt beside the car when I parked.

Patrick was anxious about parallel parking, a perceived weak area. I tried out my storehouse of sage motherly advice garnered through years of driving experience.

We reviewed his Driver's Ed instructions and I asked, "What would your teacher recommend?"

His Driver's Ed instructor was Coach Guy—a name as totally perfect as Coach Dude. It evokes images of sweaty locker rooms, high fives, and popping teammates' rumps with wet towels. The Southern equivalent might be something like Coach Sonny,

Coach Bubba, or Coach Donnie Earl, which bring to mind pickup trucks, blue tick hounds, and belching contests.

Coach Guy felt the Georgia lawmakers didn't go far enough when they adopted the new teen driving laws that had recently gone into effect.

For example, a driver under the age of eighteen cannot transport more than three nonrelated passengers in his or her car. Coach Guy said, "Just how many more passengers can you kids cram into a car, anyway?"

The teens can't get a regular license until they're eighteen. Coach Guy's response was, "If it was up to me, none of you would be driving until you're twenty-one!"

While Patrick was taking the driving portion of his exam, I remained in the waiting room observing people. One young fellow captured my attention due to his attire. He wore a Georgia Department of Corrections T-shirt and had a denim bandanna wrapped around his head. I assumed it was dual-purpose headgear, compensating for a bad hair day, plus coming in handy as a face mask for any spur of the moment armed robberies.

Surely a guardian angel would honor my malevolent prayer that this lad and my son not head out on the highways the very same day. Just in case, I rubbed my lucky penny.

Patrick aced his test and earned his highly coveted driver's license. He was eager to shuck the safe, secure cocoon of his youth. I called to include him on our insurance, at great financial sacrifice to us, his parents, I might add.

And off he drove into the sunset without glancing into the rearview mirror at the childhood he had left behind.

LANA ROBERTSON HAYES

ASHLEY

Three of the five of us in our family are adopted. For my husband and daughter, the adoption process was a smooth cruise; however, for the third member of the adoption triangle, the road was rocky—very rocky.

The decision to consider adoption began on a cloudy September morning with an innocent question from my then-nine-year-old daughter Jill.

"Mom, can we visit the Humane Society?" Wanting to please my daughter and be a good mom, I consented. Our footsteps led us like a magnet to a cage marked "Cocker-Cross." *Cocker-Cross what?* I wondered as I stared at the odd-looking puppy that gazed up at us with melancholy eyes.

The long tail and body of a beagle, cream color of a cocker spaniel, and ears and face of a golden retriever immediately confirmed her mutt heritage. At once she won our hearts. Now we had to convince my husband how much he needed to adopt this new family member. I called him on the spot.

During our conversation, I made a flippant comment: "Jill and I promise to take good care of the puppy and if it doesn't work out, we'll bring her back."

My innocent comment was overheard by the attendant, who announced as I hung up the phone, "Mrs. Fancher, we are refusing you as an adoptive mom for this puppy!"

My daughter burst into tears because I'd shattered her puppy dreams. I decided to desperately plead my case to the director. (After all, I was a pretty decent mom to my adopted daughter and wife to my husband, who was adopted.) The director decided to reconsider under one condition—that the entire family would come in and demonstrate our ability to bond with Ashley.

We arrived on Sunday dressed in our best, hoping to prove our ability to love and care for this puppy. After careful observation by staff, we passed and were awarded the privilege of raising Ashley.

Somehow my confidence in my mothering abilities faltered. Feelings of unworthiness were further confirmed on the first day, in our backyard, as Ashley dove headfirst into our pool, nearly drowning during her playful plunge.

The golden opportunity to prove that I was a competent mom presented itself in the form of an obedience school flyer. Immediately I signed Ashley and myself up for the puppy-parent boot camp. Surely the long hours spent in disciplined training would prove to me, the Humane Society, and the world that I was worthy to be called "Ashley's mom!"

Finally, the training grand finale test event arrived. Other owners and their pets appeared tense and nervous—Ashley was playful and anxiety-free, much unlike her mom. Glancing at her suspiciously, I puzzled about whether or not any training tips had registered between those floppy ears.

The evening proved to be a humiliating disaster. Ashley misinterpreted every command practiced over three months. When I commanded her to *"stay,"* she must have heard *"stray"*—sniffing and breaking the concentration of other dogs, much to the chagrin of their irate owners. When I urged *"come,"* Ashley must have heard *"run"* and bolted around the dog track like a racehorse. The audience applauded when I swept her off her paws on the tenth lap.

We received a scorecard marked with "0000" and endured the frustrated voice of our trainer: "Please control your puppy!"

As I carried Ashley through the crowd, I held my head high. Yes, I was a good mom because I'd tried my best! Ashley continues after seven years to polish, refine, and shine the puppy within. This Humane Society special remains stuck like glue to the heart we call family.

CANDIS FANCHER

*I believe that once a day people should eat together
and try to waste time,
which is not a waste of time at all.*
SOPHIA LOREN

A CHINESE BUSINESS LUNCH

M y father stood in the middle of the room, his eyes bright behind his glasses. "There's this Chinese restaurant Mom and I go to. Great food. The best soup." He bunched the tips of his fingers, brought them to his mouth, and kissed them. He extolled the egg roll, the lemon chicken, the shrimp with cashew nuts.

I feigned enthusiasm. "I know the place. The food is good."

"Would you like to go tomorrow? They have this business lunch menu."

"Great. Tomorrow."

In the evening, I found them sitting in front of the blaring TV, watching a rerun of Dallas.

"In this heat you don't eat soup, right?" my mother asked. The TV remote control is in her hand as she motions toward the world outside.

"Soup?"

"You know, at the Chinese restaurant tomorrow."

I shook my head. "No."

"In that case," she continued, "you wouldn't want to wait while we eat our soup, right?"

"No problem," I replied.

"Perhaps we should take out so you won't have to wait."

"I don't mind, really."

"But then," my mother said, "if you order a business lunch and you don't eat the soup, it will go to waste."

"Maybe I won't order the business lunch, then," I said.

"Business lunch is the best deal," my father interjected. "It has everything. But if you don't eat the soup . . . well, I don't know. . . ."

"Let's bring in, then," my mother said. "We'll eat the soup before you come home."

"It's more fun to go out and not fuss in the kitchen," I said.

"You're sure you don't mind?"

"Let's just go and enjoy ourselves," I said. "It would be fine either way." Bewilderment on her face, my mother turned her head back to the TV screen.

In the morning, next to my coffee, I found a brochure. The Chinese restaurant's menu.

"What's that for?" I asked.

"So you can decide what you'd like to order," my mother replied.

My stomach churned at the list of dishes. "It's too early," I said. "I'll stick to the usual stuff."

"You won't order the business lunch?"

I flashed her a smile. "Mom, we'll see. It's all part of the fun. We sit down, we select from the menu, I play with the chopsticks while you eat your soup. I pour us tea, we eat, we talk. Then we have fortune cookies."

At noon, dressed up for the event, they waited at the door. I drove the five-minute distance to the restaurant.

"Drop us here," my mother suggested, "and we'll order the soup while you park."

"I'll drop you off here, but don't order until I arrive," I said.

A few minutes later, I settled across the table from them. I poured the tea.

Slowly, deliberately, enjoying every sip, they ate their soup.

I watched them focus on their soup, the highlight of their day.

Pictures of my younger mother chased through my inner eye. At age thirty-two, dancing around the room in her new red skirt, swirling it until it swelled out like a parachute; age thirty-eight, the class mother on a school trip up a treacherous rocky mountainside; age forty-four, the former gym teacher performing a headstand on a high-beam.

Suddenly, I blurted, "I'll have soup, too."

It would chase away the tears that had gathered at the back of my throat.

TALIA CARNER

FINDERS KEEPERS

*E*very Easter as far back as I can remember, my parents, siblings, and I trekked to Grandma's after church. As a child I sat and fidgeted through mass picking at the waistband on my tights, in a hurry to bolt from church to Grandma's house. That's where I would find her famous banana pudding, deviled eggs, cut-glass dishes of black olives, potato salad she served in a punch bowl, Virginia-cured hams, and a selection of cakes and pies that you might expect to find in a bakery rather than on someone's sideboard.

And finally, after all that food, the Easter egg hunt.

Grandma's was no ordinary two-dozen-dyed-eggs-in-the-grass Easter egg hunt; Grandma, with my dad's help, hid over a hundred candied eggs in the backyard.

Even with the enticement of chocolate, my teen years put a damper on my enthusiasm for Grandma's Easter gathering. I was no longer small enough to jostle with the little kids for eggs, but not big enough to join the adults. On Easter morning, I'd slump in church and sulk, wishing just once I could skip Grandma's and hang out with my friends. While I loved Grandma, that whole Easter parade of family and extended family she orchestrated seemed too busy, too long, and too much. Yet every year we went, and every year in spite of myself, I wound up forgetting my misery and enjoying myself.

As a newlywed I doubted the wisdom of exposing my husband to our family's Easter insanity. I couldn't imagine how he might feel, thrust into this horde of relatives for an entire day, or how to explain Grandma's insistence that everyone, regardless of age, participate in the egg hunt. Maybe the silver dollar or lottery ticket for the most eggs found in his age group would be a lure! Maybe after a meal so magnificent, he'd be so sated, the momentum would sweep him up and carry him along without question.

As a married woman I offered to help Grandma with the cooking. I figured the time to contribute had come, but I always received the same answer.

"You all work every day, and this is my chance to cook for you."

Considering Grandma's years, I was frustrated by her refusal of help, but finally realized that preparing the Easter meal and hunt was her way of giving.

As a parent, I washed, tucked, and combed our children only to watch them squirm and pick their way through Easter service with thoughts of Great-Grandma's house spinning through them. I remember the chore of distracting them after dinner, keeping them indoors until everyone had finished eating and Grandma gave the go-ahead for the egg hunt. How Grandma, just like when I was little, handed each child his or her own official brown paper sack with the name carefully inscribed. How everyone was rousted out of the house for the hunt—no excuses. How in the end we counted eggs to see if we had them all, and sure enough, a few remained hidden. Dad and Grandma beamed with pride at their egg-hiding expertise. After scanning the yard, Dad gave hints of hot and cold until the missing eggs were found and usually slipped into some of the skimpier bags.

Grandma's annual Easter egg hunt started a tradition in which we found more than eggs. We created fond memories, treated each person with special attention, and gained family connection and joy.

This year is very different, yet very much the same. While Grandma has now passed on, her legacy survives. My mother, sister, and I are busy preparing more than one hundred special eggs, making Grandma's banana pudding, mounds of potato salad, and enjoying the smell of Virginia-cured ham coming from the oven. Each member of our growing family has a special sack for the much-anticipated Easter egg hunt.

I find myself enormously thankful for Grandma's lifelong enthusiasm, and her willingness to mold and shape a tradition of Easter renewal. We wouldn't dream of letting it go. Like all good things, strengthened with time, our Easter celebration is a sturdy thread in the weave of family that keeps us all together.

RENE B. Melton

When you come right down to it,
the secret of having it all
is loving it all.
DR. JOYCE BROTHERS

WHISPERED PRAYERS

"*Wah! Wah!*"
The shrill sound abruptly pulled me from the pleasant deep sleep that consumed me. *Maybe he'll fall back to sleep,* I groggily hoped. The crying intensified as if the baby had sensed my wish.

I was scared to open my eyes. Slowly, my head turned to the clock radio on my nightstand. The digital numbers glared at me: 3:16 A.M.

Oh no! This is the third night in a row! Why won't he sleep a full night through? This three A.M. business is getting old fast!

As I was feeling sorry for myself, I could hear that my nine-month-old baby in the next room had grasped the crib spindles and had pulled himself to a standing position, all the while sobbing as though his heart was breaking. My husband rolled over toward me to ask, "What time is it?"

"A quarter past three," I murmured.

"Do you want me to get up?"

"No, it's my turn," I irritably replied.

I was so tired! Weary to the bone, I slowly sat up on the edge of the bed before staggering toward my son's room. By now, the baby's howls were demanding, "What is taking you so long?" I couldn't determine from his frantic crying if he was experiencing pain, hunger, or thirst. I decided to start with a bottle of water to see if this would satisfy his needs.

Stumbling down the stairs and searching for a clean bottle in the dark kitchen, I quietly muttered about my lack of sleep. I could not seem to capture more than two or three hours of sleep before the baby awakened me. "Dear Lord, why is this happening? Please make him sleep! I need him to sleep if I can expect to function at school. What did I ever do to deserve nine months of interrupted sleep? Please make him fall asleep!" With that kind of attitude, it was no wonder that my prayer would go unanswered.

Yawning, I entered his bedroom. The night light cast a dim beam toward the crib. There stood my precious baby stretching his arms toward me. I lifted him out of the crib and nestled him on my lap as I sat in the rocking chair. He eagerly took the nipple and noisily sucked at the water-filled bottle.

I must have dozed off to a light sleep because I couldn't remember his finishing the entire bottle, but the last few drops of water, along with some air, were being suckled. I released the bottle from his mouth and pulled him up toward my chest to be burped. He grasped onto my neck tightly and snuggled into my shoulder. The warm feeling of unconditional love swept over me and overwhelmed me. This time it was my turn to cry. My crying wasn't the result of lost sleep mixed with frantic "How will I ever cope with these sleepless nights?" feelings. Instead, the emotions were just the opposite. I was very willing to sit there in the dead of night and slowly rock my baby and hug him. In fact, I had no desire to return to my cozy bed. All of my worries and anxieties seemed to melt, at least for a moment. I luxuriated in the oneness I felt with this tiny human being: the snuggly wrap of his arms around my neck, the tickle of his soft golden hair at my nose, his clean baby smell.

I closed my teary eyes tightly as I whispered a much more appropriate prayer: "Dear Lord, thank you for this moment."

KRISTI FRAHM

AGELESS

It was Sunday morning. My grandmother and I were getting ready for church. Lately, I've been noticing her paying a little more attention to what she was wearing, examining herself for longer periods of time in front of the mirror.

"Is everything okay, Grams?"

She checked to see if her earrings were on straight and if her blush perfectly matched the color of her pink dress.

"You have no idea what it's like."

"What what's like?"

"To be old and wrinkled."

I chuckled. "Gram, it doesn't matter what you look . . . I mean, you're . . . seventy-five!"

She turned away from me, and I immediately realized my insensitivity had hurt her feelings.

"I'm sorry. I didn't mean seventy-five in a bad way."

"Oh, it's not you I'm trying to impress."

Without speaking further, we drove the short distance to church. I felt horribly guilty, wondering if I should have told her how I really felt about her attractive appearance.

I trailed into the church behind her, while a handsome gentleman usher took her arm. Jim, a seventy-four-year-old widower often walked my grandmother down to her seat. He was so sweet to her and always made sure he saved a pew for us near the front so we could clearly see the pastor.

Then, like a lightning bolt, I understood what was really upsetting my grandmother! She wasn't depressed or really mad at me!

She was feeling insecure because she had fallen in love in her golden years.

"How are you, Loretta?" Jim inquired.

"Well."

"My brother came for a surprise visit," Jim explained.

"I'm sorry I missed you at bingo. I heard you won, though. Congratulations."

I scooted down into our pew, determining that Jim must have been asking about my grandmother's whereabouts on Wednesday as well.

Tenderly gazing down into her dark brown eyes, he escorted her to my side. After holding her hand for a brief moment, he shakily pulled a crumbled piece of paper out of his pocket and placed it in her hand.

I waited until he walked away. "What does it say, Grams?"

She blushed. "It has his phone number and says to call him if I'd like to go to the singles dance on Saturday."

I fought back tears of joy, witnessing her brilliant smile wipe away all signs of wrinkles.

"See, someone else knows how beautiful you are too, Grams; you're still as perfect as you ever were."

"He just needs a dancing partner, that's all."

I countered. "Gram, he wants to waltz with someone who cares about him."

Her face lit up. "Maybe you're right."

"I know I am."

Watching my grandmother and Jim dance that night was something that took my breath away. My husband, Louis, and I were worried about her and decided to drop by. With one glance, all our fears disappeared. They were swinging like teenagers, laughing and holding each other underneath the twinkle of the stars.

Nine months later, at the age of seventy-four, Jim dropped

down onto one knee and asked for my seventy-five-year-old grandmother's hand in marriage.

"Yes," she immediately replied. "But . . . there's just one thing."

"What's that?" Jim wiped the tears from her rosy cheeks.

"I don't do windows anymore."

He clapped with excitement. And before a man of God, my family and I came together, filling His house to watch them wed by candlelight.

It's been eight years now and Jim and Loretta are still just as happy as the night they danced until dawn. Every time I see them together, I'm reminded that love is ageless. It's as priceless at eighty as it is at twenty, perhaps even more.

Louis and I often stop by their house to visit. Grandma always has an apple pie waiting for us. And Jim, well, he's usually the one doing the housework. I don't think it bothers him though; he too has learned a valuable lesson. Love mends all things: doubts, age, the differences between generations, even a lonely fellow's heart that wanted a new start.

MICHELE WALLACE CAMPANELLI

GOODBYE, MY SON

I have always prided myself on going toward the light. I look for joy in the darkest of places, and it was with great surprise that I found myself reacting to a very joyous event with uncharacteristic melancholy.

My son is getting married. My firstborn—my soul mate—my joy. From the moment of his birth, we bonded—a glue of laughter and shared sensibilities that has held us together through the terrible twos and the turbulent teens. Almost six feet tall, self-supporting, independent, he is a man I rely on still to make me laugh and make me feel that I did an O.K. job as a parent.

He is leaving me for another woman—young, gorgeous, tall, blond, blue-eyed, and with legs up to her neck. Funny, bright, caring—the most perfect woman a mother could ever wish for her son. She loves him with such purity, it makes my eyes fill sometimes, just to see them together. He treats her with such gentleness and generosity that I marvel at what an incredible man he has become.

And yet I grieve. Not for the impending nuptials, but for the time past. A time when the only woman he ever wanted or needed was me. I am no longer his mommy—I am his mom. I can no longer pull him up on my lap and comfort him. I can no longer protect him from life or the bogeyman.

I am glad he has grown so well, and I am glad he has found the one—the perfect one—for him. I am proud that I have given him wings to fly and not an anchor to secure him in safe harbors only—but oh, how I miss that little boy.

I accept the fact that all things change and that someday he will have children of his own. I know I will adjust to being a former mommy and I look forward to the day that I will answer to Grandma, but I don't think I will ever stop missing those golden days, when it was just him and me and all the time in the world.

JUDI SADOWSKY

IV

TELLING IT LIKE IT IS

Behind every successful woman . . .

is a substantial amount of coffee.

STEPHANIE PIRO

ENGLISH AS A
SECOND LANGUAGE

I *didn't know that I could have a stroke in my early* thirties. When I was released from the hospital five days later, the doctor's discharge instructions to me were to "go and live your life." With no regard to fatigue, disorientation, and my speech deficits, I decided to do what a normal person would do on December 23. I went Christmas shopping. At the mall!

It became apparent that my expressive speech was a problem. Word finding and a limited vocabulary at my disposal made descriptions of potential purchases almost impossible. My gestures became so important that pantomime was the primary way I communicated. My New York upbringing seemed to save the day.

But I couldn't ignore the puzzled and sometimes horrified looks on the harried sales clerks' faces when I made my requests for assistance. Their thoughts were obvious. Was I crazy, or just drunk? I needed a new plan. I decided that the truth was the best course and at the next few stores, I began each conversation with what seemed to me a simple and slow explanation. "I had stroke. I want buy presents. Please."

This was even worse! The look of sadness was overwhelming. Nobody wants to think of sickness and impairment in a young person, especially at Christmastime. And the sadness was often replaced by pity. Ish! Time again for yet another plan.

I approached the next store clerk and smiled. Not even trying for the right words, I said, "I talk French. I want buy presents. Please." I didn't even try for an accent—it wasn't necessary. My broken, faltering English proved that English was a second language for me. My little speech was accepted with smiles, help, and encouragement. Amazingly, I was complimented about my "good English." I smiled modestly whenever that happened.

This trick worked so well that my shopping was almost complete in short order. Soon, I was at the last store, giving yet another overwhelmed clerk my "French" spiel. However, this young lady's response was different. She listened carefully and answered my questions, but she seemed surprised and even a little shocked.

Only when I left the store did my friend start laughing hysterically. In between choking and gasping gales of laughter, did she fill me in. "Next time," she said, "make sure the sales clerk is not French."

HOLLY NOELLE SCHAEFER

If you want breakfast in bed, sleep in the kitchen.
AUTHOR UNKNOWN

A VICTORIOUS
TUG OF WAR

We'd waited for two years for my ex-husband to come see us in our new home. Don't get me wrong. Tony wasn't avoiding us. We wrote, called, and sent appropriate cards for holidays and birthdays. It's just that we had not been near each other in two years. We lived in separate states.

I wondered if he would bring his girlfriend. But, no, he had said, "I'm coming," not, "We're coming." So I was pretty sure he would be coming alone. Stray thoughts would enter my mind. *Will he want to sleep with me? Will he be kind or strict with the children? Will we end up arguing?* I shot down all the stray thoughts. I was going to take this a minute at a time. *Why am I so nervous?*

Time was not something that I had had a lot of since I had returned to college. Getting my degree was important to me. I was doing something for myself. Of course, the children would benefit from the better job, with the better pay and the benefits. When that day came, we'd no longer need public assistance. We might even have our own home, instead of living in public housing.

It was almost time for him to arrive. I should have asked him what color car he was driving. The make and model meant nothing to me. All cars were either small, medium, or large—pickup or, my kids' preference, a mini-van. When he did arrive, in a black medium-sized Chevy, the children greeted him with emotions and laughter fit to welcome a king. He ate it up too. It never occurred to me that he might be nervous; that he might think that his visit would not be welcomed. But the look on his face was more than happiness; it expressed relief.

The children took him on a tour of the house, showing off their possessions and the prominent places where his gifts were being displayed. I tried to stay in the background. This visit was more for the children than for me.

I got out my business law text to study. It was my intention to do well on the midterm the next day. My average in that class was ninety-five, and I intended to keep it that way. Besides the boost in my morale, getting good grades inspired my children to do better. When they saw how serious I was about education for myself, they gave me the impression that they, too, would take their education more seriously. Their grades were improving. A visit from their father was not going to diminish the need to study and prepare for an exam. I knew the children would be watching me.

Tony came back into the living room and sat next to me on the couch. "Well, what's for dinner? I drove a long way. Oh, by the way, I've decided to spend the night."

Not with me you're not! I thought. "O.K. We've got enough room for one more. But I have an exam to study for, so it will have to be Kentucky Fried or Hardees for dinner."

Tony's eyebrows rose, exposing that little scar over his right eye. His patrician nose flared, as he said, "You're going to get up off your ass and get in that kitchen and cook me some chicken. I don't eat Kentucky Fried or Hardees." Then he just stared at me, daring me to defy him.

It's starting again, and it hasn't even been an hour. I'm not going to let him come into my home for the first time and take over as if we'd never been apart. I straightened my spine and stared him right back in the face. "No! You listen to me. I have an exam to study for. So, if you want fresh chicken for dinner I'll tell you what you can do. You can go to the supermarket and buy the chicken. Then you can come back here. I give you *my* permission to go into *my* kitchen and cook it. It's either that or you can go up to Hardees or Kentucky Fried. That is your choice."

Tony's body jerked as if I'd slapped him. This was not the response he'd been prepared for. His mouth fell open as if to speak, but no words came out. *I'd always loved that mouth.* He got up and walked out of the house, calling to the children to come with him to Hardees. With the battle over for the moment, they were more than glad to leave the house.

After dinner I told him, in front of the kids, that he'd sleep in our ten-year-old's room in one of the bunk beds. The kids would tuck him in and wake him in the morning. *I have no intention of letting him sleep in my bed.* From the slight slump of his shoulders, I realized that he got my message. *I wanted him. We had some good memories. But the price was too high!*

As at other times when events baffled me, I sought out my psych instructor. I was confused after my ex-husband's visit. Had he changed and gotten harder? Was he always this way? Or was I seeing him in a different light? Maybe I had changed. I wasn't sure.

"I doubt very much that he has changed," she said. "He was probably used to talking to you that way. You've changed. You are now seeing him the way he is instead of the way you wanted him to be. You probably made excuses for him whenever he talked to you like that before."

She was right. I'd always excused his attitude and gruffness because I thought he was tired from working so hard. It never occurred to me when we were together before that the way he talked to me was wrong. My father had always talked like that to my mother, so to me, it was normal. I didn't know any other way, except in the movies. That is when it became clear to me how abuse is carried down from one generation to another.

That night I cried after getting into bed. There was a time when I idolized my ex-husband. He was so handsome. He knew how to make me feel really good. But, that was only a physical good. There was never any respect shown by him for my mind, my thoughts. That's when I was "stupid." I remembered the times I'd stood up for myself. Then he'd turn his back on me when we got into bed, ignoring my touch. He knew that would hurt me. That was his way of punishing me for disagreeing with him.

But it was so good that it was over. Not only the emotional tug of war—but the abuse. The children would no longer have that as an example to follow. There would now be a break in that cycle. Just thinking of that took away a lot of the pain I'd felt. My children would no longer see me cry from sorrow. Their mother is now stronger and emotionally more stable. I've set goals that I know I can achieve. The examples I set before them are positive ones. I'm more at peace with myself than I've been for a very, very long time.

BETH DUNCAN

If you obey all the rules you miss all the fun.
KATHERINE HEPBURN

HEATING UP THE OFFICE

I've worked for years for a large corporation that does not have a great reputation for being employee-oriented. Recently, the top executives distributed a long employee survey, and they were shocked by the largely negative employee response. Morale was low!

Management talked about launching a campaign to show employees it cared. We were asked what we wanted. Some of our ideas: a bonus, a free day off, holiday celebrations, a turkey at Thanksgiving, and employee recognition awards.

Meanwhile, memos were being posted throughout the building:

Notice: Space Heaters

Individual space heaters are not allowed unless deemed a special circumstance due to a medical condition. Special circumstances would require a doctor's note stating that it is for the associate to use a space heater because of a medical condition.

When I walked into the break room and saw the notice posted, my heart sank. I love my space heater. When I need heat, I turn it on. I do this frequently. It's been one of the best investments I've ever made. I'm in control of the temperature in my office, and I like it that way. I learned that buying my own space heater was the answer to the temperature problems that run rampant through our building.

This was a worrisome development. I decided the best thing to do for my stress level was to ignore it. And I did so, happily, until one day, two weeks later, the Safety Committee chairwoman marched into my office and dropped a new memo on my desk.

"You're not going to like this," she warned, and walked out. The memo read:

Important Notice!!!

In recent days we have been walking around the building and noticed many space heaters in various cubicles. Space heaters are not allowed unless deemed as a special circumstance due to a medical condition. Special circumstances require a doctor's note.

At lunch that day two coworkers and I discussed the space heater problem. It bothered me that I would have to get a doctor's note to keep the space heater I've had for two years. I didn't want to ask my doctor to lie for me, and I couldn't think of a medical condition that would require a space heater! So I wrote my own doctor's note, hoping the company would get the hint.

To: Safety Committee Chairwoman
From: Herr Medical Provider, M.D.
Dear Safety Committee Chairwoman:

My patient, Melanie Caster, otherwise healthy female Caucasian, age thirty-four, average build, asked me to provide you with a physician's note, which is required to allow her to keep her space heater.

My patient is afflicted with a rare medical disorder called C.O.L.D. The Latin term is unpronounceable, but in essence, it means "Chilled on the Lower Decks." This malady primarily affects her legs and feet and the symptoms, for some mysterious reason, seem to disappear in the summer months.

After numerous tests, we have concluded that this medical problem is a result of temperatures dipping below what is comfortable to her person. The symptoms appear to be cold, stiff fingers, which make it difficult for her to use her keyboard, and cold feet, which make her an unhappy worker. Unfortunately, her business attire requires she wear heels, nylons, and skirts rather than wool slacks, wool socks, and boots. Because my patient is cold-blooded and thin-skinned, the C.O.L.D. disease is especially dangerous to her well-being.

We have researched various treatments for this diagnosis. During the past few years, we have enlisted the help of a well-known heat specialist, Dr. Facilities Department. However, quality control and differences of opinion differ greatly between my patient, who spends several hours a day in her office, and Dr. Facilities, who passes through on occasion and deems the office "warm enough." My patient has noted that she is not the only person in the vicinity who is afflicted with C.O.L.D. So, taking matters into her own hands, being the good health consumer that she is and a terrific doctor's partner, she purchased her very own space heater, which allows her to control the temperature as she deems necessary. My patient believes she has shown responsible behavior with her space heater thus far and promises to continue doing so.

It is under these special circumstances that I submit this doctor's note stating that this associate be allowed to keep her space heater, which is equipped with the required safety features.

Sincerely,
Herr Medical Provider, M.D.

The note quickly made its way around the office. The Safety Committee chairwoman loved it and told me I was writing the wrong kind of material. (Don't I know it! I write marketing materials for the company.) She asked for permission to share it with others on the committee and with the Facilities Department. She showed it to another woman who was perplexed about what medical excuse she could use to get her doctor to write her a note. I was told the Facilities Department worried about the note being real.

A week later my supervisor reminded me that I needed a "real" note.

Egads! How much more honest could I be? I was being forced to ask my doctor to write a false note. I couldn't do it. So I took my original note to my doctor. Not only did he sign it; he copied it on his letterhead and added his phone number below his signature. My doctor's note was now official!

I submitted my "real" doctor's note and never heard another word about it. My space heater and I still hang out together on those C.O.L.D. chilly days, heating up the office.

MELANIE ANDERSON-CASTER

DIVAS!

There's something in us
that whistles like a kid,
walking free on a country road.

There's something in us
that builds things—
like the sun rises.

There's something in us
that speaks, like the ocean's
gentle thunder.

There's something in us
that directs our life
like an inspired maestro.

There's something in us
that is a symphony,
at one with the stars.

There's something in us
that sees us all
as part of the Milky Way—

All divas, in training!
All learning to remember

our beauty and our strength,
so we might answer wisdom's call—

and whistle
whole new worlds
into sweet
existence.

SHEILA STEPHENS

LIFE'S NOT FAIR

Steven comes out of the bathroom and finds me folding the wash. With his mouth open, his braces blocking my view, and his words garbled because he's speaking with his finger pointing at something inside his mouth, he says, "See?"

"See what?"

"My tooth is gone," he says. He reopens his mouth to point once again at the space.

"Yup, looks it."

"I think I swallowed it in my sleep," he says.

"Or when you were eating."

"I would have known if I swallowed it when I was eating."

"Probably. Did you check in your bed?"

"Already did that."

"Well, then it's gone."

"Do I get money anyway?"

"I don't think so. Think the Tooth Fairy needs the tooth."

"Mo-o-om," he says in a three-syllable stretch.

I know he's known almost from the first tooth who the Tooth Fairy is. I'm not even sure he ever believed in the fantasy. It's one of the hazards of being the youngest sibling. Older kids always spoil the fantasies way too soon.

"But that's not fair." He doesn't wait for my response. "I know. I know. Life's not fair. But that's not fair."

"It still could be in your stomach. You could still get it." I'm laughing at him as I continue to fold some towels.

"Mom, that's gross."

"Well, you could."

"Mo-o-o-m."

"Only a suggestion."

Steven sulks out of the room, unaware that the Tooth Fairy will be visiting his pillow anyway. I hear him down the hall discussing the lost tooth with his dad.

"But, Da-a-a-d," he says, "that's not fair." Then I hear him say, "You're just as gross as Mom."

Later in the day I observe Steven pointing into his mouth showing his brother the space. His brother shrugs, and goes back to the Nintendo game he's engrossed in.

Steven sulks down the hall to his room.

"You're not gonna stiff him, Mom. Are you?" his brother asks.

"Why are you asking me?" I say. "Do I look like the Tooth Fairy?"

"Come on, Mom. That's not fair. I always got money for my teeth."

Shocked at his brotherly concern, I look at him cross-eyed. "You always had a tooth to give the Tooth Fairy."

"That's not fair."

"Life's not fair." I snap off the TV. "Now, go make your bed and clean up your room."

"Mom! I was in the middle of a game."

"Life's not fair. Now go clean your room."

My daughter does us a favor and joins us for dinner. Now that she has her license and her own car, she "visits" with us, on occasion.

"Let me see, Stevie," she says. She's the only one who gets away with calling him this nickname. He opens his mouth. There is still food in it, but he points to the space anyway.

Across the table, my other son says, "Gross. Finish swallowing first, pig."

My daughter is more indulgent. "What's that now? Like nine teeth?"

"Uh huh," Steven answers, "but this one isn't going under my pillow. I can't find it. It's gone."

"I'm sure the Tooth Fairy will visit anyway. Maybe you should write her a note. Good idea, Mom?" She is staring at me, as if teasing, as if being in on a secret, a great conspiracy.

"Waste of time," I say. "No tooth. Tooth Fairy wants a tooth."

"Mom, that's not fair." She looks toward my husband for support.

"Life's not fair," he says.

Before we go to sleep, my husband hands me an 1887 silver dollar to put under Steven's pillow. My husband has a few of these old silver dollars he's been saving for special occasions. It's been a tough day for Steven.

The house is quiet. I slip into Steven's room. He is a sound sleeper. I slide my hand under his pillow to leave the silver dollar and I feel paper rustling. Thinking he left the Tooth Fairy a note, I pull it out, and I leave Steven to dream with the special treasure under his pillow.

I get into my bed to share the note with my husband. I'm sure it's going to be charming. We're both already charmed by the fact that Steven has put his note in an envelope.

On the outside of the envelope, in my daughter's handwriting, it says, "You don't need a tooth. I knew anyway!" She signs it, "The Tooth Fairy" with a heart over the "i."

There is a P.S. in our older son's handwriting, "Don't chew with your mouth open. It's gross." We hold the envelope up to the light to see what's inside; it looks like a two-dollar-bill.

"Where'd they get that?" I say aloud.

My husband takes the envelope from me. "Don't you remember? That's what we used to leave for *them* when *they* lost their teeth."

"But now Steven's getting three dollars," I say.

"Life's not fair," my husband says as he goes down the hall to put the envelope back under Steven's pillow.

FELICE R. PRAGER

ADOPTION DAY

I *smiled at him, pretending it was just another day,* but the solemn man seated across from me was fiddling with his paisley tie, cracking his knuckles, and acting every bit the part of an expectant father.

His wife stared out the window in silence.

The birth mother was on the other side of the closed door, seated at the hallway table, signing papers to irreconcilably relinquish her six-week-old son for adoption. It was my task to keep the adoptive parents cornered in the small office until the social worker arrived to present their new family member to them.

As the minutes ticked by, the adoptive mother sat down, and we chatted about nothing in particular. The adoptive father took his turn at the window to watch the leafless trees lining the city street five stories below us.

After an uncomfortable lull in our conversation, the adoptive mother-to-be announced, "I need to go to the bathroom." Her tone was urgent.

I flinched. "Sorry, the birth mother is out there. You've got to stay in here, please." I smiled encouragingly at her, "I'm sure it won't be much longer."

"But I have to . . ."

I shook my head, feeling like a prison warden. "Not yet. Please try to be patient. You know you can't see her."

I sighed. My boss would kill me if the adoptive mother jogged out into the hallway and came face-to-face with the young birth mother who needed these precious minutes to say an emotional goodbye to the infant she would probably never again see. This was to be an incognito adoption process, agreed to in writing by all parties.

"The social worker will be here soon with your little guy."

She nodded. Then I heard a gasp. Red-faced, she stood up, urine streaming down her legs, running into her designer pumps and onto the moss green carpet. She stared down in horror, speechless.

Her husband rushed to her side, wrapped both his arms around his wife, and began rocking her gently, crying. "Honey, it's going to be all right. Our new son is just outside that door. Our long wait is almost over." He kissed his wife's hair, her eyebrows, her nose, his tears running down to his chin.

The more he cried, the more she peed.

I stared at the scene unfolding before my eyes. This was the twenty-eighth adoption I'd been involved with at the agency, but nothing had prepared me for anything like this.

He clutched his wife's hands. "You're a beautiful mother." He had meanwhile stopped crying, and she had seemingly stopped peeing. His rocking had turned into a quasi-waltzing motion, and he twirled her around the tiny office, diplomatically skirting the wet spot on the carpet.

"We'll be fine, the three of us. All we've got to do is put him into his little car seat, carefully drive home, and take it from there. Everything's going to be perfect."

Not knowing what else to do, I continued to stare at the dancing couple. Ideas flashed through my brain. I couldn't go to the utility room to get a bucket of water because I'd been instructed not to leave the room under any circumstances. The desk phone was locked, so I couldn't call any coworkers for help. Politely I handed out tissues from the social worker's desk as the couple spun by me. I smiled as brightly as I could manage.

I was ready for a way out, but my only escape hatch, the door, remained off limits. I opened the window wide and faced the brisk October day. Moments later, my rescue knock sounded at the door, the tension dissipated immediately, and we all broke out in grins. I offered a wave to the thrilled new parents and was again a free woman.

ROBERTA BEACH JACOBSON

Well-behaved women rarely make history.
LAUREL THATCHER ULRICH

A PICTURE IS WORTH A THOUSAND WORDS

*T*he rift in our family occurred when I was seven years old, and the result left my family divided by anger and bitterness for years. My sister, who was nineteen, was leaving an abusive husband. My parents, concerned about her ability to support her infant son, testified against her at the custody hearing. In deep pain and sorrow, my sister fled over half the state away to take refuge with Mom's mother, brother, and sister-in-law.

At first, my sister's whereabouts were unknown, and my mother was beside herself. She withdrew into an emotional fortress, bolstering her solitude with alcohol. She allowed no one inside. When she finally unearthed my sister's whereabouts, she was livid and vowed to disown both my sister and her own mother in retaliation.

Years passed before we saw my sister again, and then only under very strained circumstances. She had remarried and given birth to a beautiful baby girl. Reluctantly, Mom allowed them into our lives, but any mention of Grandma or my uncle's family was taboo.

With encouragement from my sister, the rest of the family began to secretly visit the shunned relatives. I discovered I'd missed growing up with some warm, caring, intelligent people. The joy of these visits, however, had a downside in that they had to be made on the sly to avoid Mom's wrath.

Once Grandma turned eighty, her health began to decline. I became concerned that my mother might regret their estrangement if Grandma passed away. One fall day, when the reds and yellows of the leaves pierced the crisp blue sky, I sat at a sunny window with Mom and told her of Grandma's poor health. The cords in her neck tightened and her breathing shallowed before she erupted in a defensive fury, giving me endless reasons she could never speak with Grandma again. She drew my father into the conversation, only to become more agitated when he sided with me.

"Mom, you don't have to forgive Grandma," I said, "or even forget about the things that happened, but you do need to at least see her. You owe it to yourself—if not to Grandma—to at least speak with her before she dies."

My mother was up and pacing the floor by this point and headed straight for a bottle of wine. I gave up in frustration and went home thinking that was that. But by some miracle, she phoned Grandma the next day.

That holiday season, after my sister became a grandmother, she flew into town to meet the new arrival and visit with her daughter and son-in-law. Grandma wanted to see the new baby too. We weren't sure that she could manage the four-hour car trip, but she was determined to see her great-great-granddaughter. I phoned my mother to let her know Grandma would be coming.

"I wanted to give you fair warning since there's a chance you might run into her," I said.

A moment of silence passed before my mother said, "Can she stay with us?"

Our relatives were dumbstruck when I announced our plans.

"Your mom and grandma in the same house? You can't be serious!" they said.

But when I pulled alongside the curb in front of Mom's house with Grandma, Mom took Grandma by the arm and gently led her inside. It had been twenty-five years since the two of them had seen one another.

Since we'd gotten this far, I decided to take things one step farther. Knowing that a picture is worth a thousand words, I arranged to have all the women sit together for studio portraits. The four adults took turns holding the newborn for the camera, and the smiles captured were all from the heart. Later we joined the rest of the family for an impromptu reunion.

Less than three months later, a stroke claimed my mother at age sixty-four. I'm so grateful that I found the courage when I did to talk to her about something that so deeply mattered.

Now each time I glance at my treasured, five-generation photograph, I see individual women who all cared in their own special ways, and I see all of us brought back together—just in time—to seal the family bond.

DENA McCLUNG

MOMENTS OF TRUTH

My *six-and-a-half-year-old son, Ron, and his four-year-old sister, Marly,* bolted into the living room with such force that they almost knocked each other over.

"Mom," Ron reported breathlessly, "Carl's grandma just told us that we came from way up in heaven to live with you and Daddy. Is that true? Really?" Two sets of brown eyes looked at me, burning a hole in the air with the urgency of their question.

Ron and Carl were the same age, and Carl's grandmother had become the most quoted authority in our household on matters ranging from oatmeal cookies to puppy training and weather forecasts. I was quick to decide that her most recent pearl of wisdom was not going to join the ranks of Grandma Ecker's contributions cherished by my children.

Memories of my own childhood and confused early teens flashed vividly in my mind. I had been raised with the same kind of fairy tale my children had just heard. In my case, it was the comfortable falsehood about the stork's door-to-door delivery system. Later, dark, hushed secrets, innuendoes, half-truths, and crude jokes became the other unreliable sources of information.

I wasn't going to let that happen to my children. I wanted to be sure they heard about the subject of sex in a way that promoted wonder and awe at the process, and conveyed the message of privilege and responsibility. I never understood why parents who taught their children good manners, ethics, and everything else for life, shied away from sex education and preferred strangers to do that important job for them.

I hauled out a book I had purchased long ago in preparation for the moment of clarification, sat the two kids down, and started to tell them the magical story of life. Ron and Marly had long ago learned to call all their body parts by their proper names—we never referred to their private parts as "thingies" or "what-cha-ma-call-its." That was the natural thing to do. And so was what followed.

Slowly, easily, and simply, the story of life unfolded itself. Together, we looked at the pictures in the children's book that illustrated the "technical" part of procreation, and I told them about the changes their little bodies would go through over the years before all that could happen. We talked about how one day they would be grown up and finished with school. Each of them would drive a car, have a job, earn a living, have a bank account. They would know a lot more about the world and about themselves. They might be married (bouts of giggles) and perhaps have children.

I was surprised at their undivided attention to the story. Busy Ron and wiggly Marly remained riveted to their seats. They loved the part about having lived inside their mother and were fascinated with the illustrations that depicted an embryo in the various stages of development. When I tucked them into their beds that night, Marly pleaded, "Mommy, tell us the story again about the time we lived in your body."

"That's really neat," Ron joined his sister, "how we lived inside you and how we came out. Wow! I better tell Carl's grandma. She doesn't know that!"

That was my cue to reemphasize the privacy factor: we don't talk about such private things. We don't tell the neighbors how much money we make; we don't discuss family matters and other personal things. Their faces serious, both kids nodded in agreement.

When I chatted with my husband that evening, I glowed and crowed about what a wonderful day it had been. How well the story of life had told itself, how bright the children, and how easy it had been to tackle that age-old hush-hush subject. He was delighted but a bit apprehensive about the children sharing their newly acquired information with others.

"Oh no. We talked a lot about privacy," I assured him. Well, I should have known better.

A week later, my six-year-old replied to a visitor's comment of how he was getting to be as big as his father with: "Gee, Mr. Frame, maybe I'm getting as tall as my dad, but my penis sure isn't as big as his yet." *Thanks, buddy!* (He had surprised his father, who had neglected to lock the door to the bathroom.)

A few days later, Marly informed the mailman that I couldn't come to the door because: "Mommy is menstrufating." *Thank you, little sis!* The mailman fled down the steps as though the devil were on his tail, and never again rang our doorbell—even if he had to pay the pennies on my overdue postage from his own pocket.

Once again, we went into a huddle and discussed what I called "the story-of-life privacy promise." All went well until my son was playing with a neighbor girl in the back and it started to rain. He bounced into the kitchen to announce that he and Molly were heading for the basement playroom. "We're going to play make a baby."

I quickly grabbed him, sat him down at the kitchen table, and asked him what it took to become a father. He thought about it for a second, and the light went on in his eyes. "Oh, yeah. I don't have a job. I don't drive a car. I don't have any money. I don't . . ."

With that, he slid off the chair, opened the door that led to the basement, and yelled down, "Hey, Molly, we're going to have to play something else!"

Oh dear! What next? I wondered. Well, I didn't have to wait long.

In spite of my relentless instructions not to talk about "private matters," chatty, little Marly had taken it upon herself to teach her five-year-old friend Jenny the proper names for the parts of our bodies. The result was a knock on my door.

Jenny's mother, my neighborhood friend, appeared a bit edgy and agitated when she said, "Your Marly can no longer play with my Jenny. Your daughter told my little girl that she had a . . . uh, she had a . . ." Beet-red faced and embarrassed, she stuttered on, "that Jenny had a . . . a . . . vagina." There! She finally got that terrible word out.

"Oh, my dear," I replied, lacing my voice with astonishment and false concern, "don't tell me Jenny doesn't have one. Why, that's terrible!"

My friend didn't think that was funny and left in a huff. When she appeared at my door two days later, I was prepared to apologize for my bratty retort. But to my great surprise and delight, she wanted to borrow the books I had used to tell my children about the story of life and asked me how to get started.

Being a mother is a great job—especially when you *know* you've done something right.

URSULA BACON

V
CREATING A NEW REALITY

You don't need a crystal ball to see your future,

you just need to look at the choices

you are making.

KAREN SHERIDAN

FULL THROTTLE

*L*ast *Saturday, my husband and I went snowmobiling* for my birthday. I was so excited, I had been half-packed for a week. A whole day of fun in the snow was a needed break. We set off early for the hour and a half drive. Fresh powder had fallen the night before, and everything was frosted white. The sun sparkled on the snow and the trails were completely empty. I was thrilled we'd be the only people for miles.

Until we got going.

Suddenly, my excitement melted into fear. I had no idea why, or where it was coming from, but every turn, every hill, every steep climb of the mountain scared me to death. I kept picturing crashing headlong into a tree, or falling off the side of a drop. My hands grew clammy inside my gloves and my heart pounded. I couldn't wait to be finished and safe inside the nice warm lodge. As the path became rougher, I shouted at my husband that we were really "mogul-mobiling," a term that suited the sport. My fear deepened.

Periodically, my husband would turn around and holler, "Wanna drive now?" I would shout back, *"No!"* over the roar of the engine and hope that he wouldn't ask again.

Finally, we finished the first trail and took a break. Over lunch, I confessed my irrational fear to my husband. As usual, he made me feel more calm and less phobic as we talked about it. I decided to focus on the beauty around me.

Back on the trails, I willed myself to relax and started spotting deer tracks in the fresh powder. I felt myself smile at the incredible beauty and solitude that we were being blessed with that day. Sharing a mountain with nothing but wildlife is a rare occurrence, and I began to take in and enjoy the pure wonder around us.

My husband somehow sensed my fear melting away and began to open up and fly like the wind. I saw the huge unmistakable tracks of a bear whiz by and grinned at the thought of a bear watching us zip past him.

I began to regret being afraid to drive. Deep down, I really wanted to be in charge of the thing that scared me. And it made me mad that I was afraid to do something I really wanted to do.

I signaled to my husband to pull over, and we took a breather and snapped some pictures of the pristine scenery surrounding us.

With a sense of adventure growing within me, I walked over to the edge of the trail where the fresh snow was deep, flung my arms wide, and with a giggle, let myself fall straight back into the snow. Waving my arms and legs, I made my first snow angel. I got up and my husband and I admired what was truly the most perfect snow angel we had ever seen. Pleased with myself and giddy with the silliness of it all, I began to think that maybe—just maybe—I could drive the snowmobile after all. Saying nothing to my husband, I climbed on behind him and we hit the trail once again.

Our day was coming to an end, and the lodge was not too far away. I knew that if I didn't take my chance now, the opportunity would be lost.

Signaling for my husband to pull over, I announced that I was ready to drive. Heart pounding, I started off slowly and felt the wind in my face. Then I sped up a little more. My hair was flying straight out behind me. I heard myself let out a little squeal that revealed both fear and excitement. I stood up on the snowmobile and surveyed the trail ahead of me. Deciding that I was going full out, I let out a loud whoop and opened the throttle. I took my husband on the best bone-crunching, teeth-cracking, butt-busting ride of the day. I heard his laughter over the engine and grinned at my newly discovered wild streak.

We ended the day on a breathless, carefree note, and I was proud of myself. It's not every day that a body can conquer fear. But I did. I also learned a valuable lesson or two. Forcing myself to experience something scary that I really wanted to do gave me a sense of power, a sense of being able to overcome other obstacles in my life.

I've never liked the times when I've thought, *"I wish I had."* This time, I replaced it with *"I'm glad I did!"* Squelching my fears also allowed me to calm down enough to see, *really* see the beauty around me.

At the ripe old age of thirty-five, I'm now looking forward—with a little bit of fear and a lot of excitement—to the next thrill life has to offer. And you're never too old for that.

SUSAN FARR-FAHNCKE

CUTTING HER LOSSES

*L*eslie has *always been one of my low-risk clients. I* own my own hair salon and over the years, I've noticed that my customers are fairly predictable with their preferred hairstyles.

If someone were to ask me about individual clients and how willing each is to take a risk with a new hairstyle, I could break my customers down into three broad categories. Some love to keep up with all the latest styles and cuts. Others want to know what's in fashion, and they may let me cut a little at a time over a period of months. A few of the ladies choose to stick with the same cut no matter what.

Leslie falls into the last category. I really don't blame her. Her beautiful, thick light brown hair naturally falls loosely onto her shoulders in soft curls. All I need to do is give her a quick trim every couple of months.

Recently, before Leslie's last appointment, I spotted her out the window standing in front of her car in the parking lot deep in conversation with another woman. She's always had a playful nature, but her body language wasn't the same. Instead of the carefree swing that was vintage Leslie, she appeared tense and serious and close to tears.

"Do we need to reschedule your appointment?" I asked when she walked into the salon toward my station.

"LaVonne, we need to do something different today," she responded. "I just left the doctor's office and found out that I need to have a double mastectomy in five days and heavy chemotherapy after that."

My heart sank as our eyes met. Her news was every woman's worst nightmare. Even though I felt helpless, I wanted to find a way to help.

"Well, maybe we should cut your hair shorter today, Leslie."

"Yeah, I was thinking a Sharon Stone look."

I knew what she meant. She wanted to feel that in some way she could regain some control over her circumstances.

Fueled by Leslie's idea, a lovely vision appeared in my mind's eye as I toweled the moisture from her hair: a woman looking very powerful and sure of herself. Leslie was right—the timing was perfect for her to take charge of her life. We both knew that if I just trimmed a little bit, she would have more to lose once her chemotherapy began. It would fall out slowly for a few weeks after the first treatments, then in clumps. With her long hair, it might scare her to see so much coming out at once on her pillow, in her hairbrush, and in the shower.

"If you're going after a Sharon Stone look, let's do it right!"

A smile grew wide across Leslie's face. She was back in charge. She even became playful, asking me to turn her away from the mirror so that she could be surprised later. Ceremoniously, neither one of us spoke while I fingered her long hair, then picked up my scissors.

A number of the other customers and stylists glanced our way when they saw Leslie's beautiful hair falling to the floor, but for the most part, it was just the two of us enjoying a special time together in silence. By the time I finished her cut and color, she'd been in the chair for an hour and a half.

Leslie's eyes opened very wide when I turned the chair around and she looked at her reflection in the mirror. For a woman who rarely makes changes, this one was drastic and wonderful at the same time. She looked at herself and saw a Sharon Stone look-alike. Leslie looked drop-dead gorgeous with her bleached blond buzz cut, and colorful makeup.

"My kids are going to love this," she said, grinning. "You know, LaVonne, once my hair falls out completely, I'm going to wear turbans, and I expect my husband to buy me the Hope diamond."

Not long after, I was reading the Sunday paper at home and there on the society page was a picture of Leslie elegantly dressed for a formal affair wearing a turban with a beautiful jewel in the center. The caption read, "Who could look this beautiful in a turban?" Certainly, a woman fully in her power no matter what life sends her way.

LAVONNE HOLLAND

LAUNCHING A DREAM
ON LOBSTERS

*D*efining moments are not supposed to occur in the local fish market. Rather, they should be created on a wedding day, during the birth of a child, or at a long-awaited graduation. In addition, these life-altering experiences are supposed to be planned for, anticipated, or at least somewhat expected.

However, as I walked to our neighborhood fishery with my husband of twenty years, a sense of foreboding overshadowed me. I kept thinking, something is up, and I don't know that I want to hear it. With seagulls squawking overhead and water lapping against the shore, he told me that he wanted to leave his job. Break out on his own. Live by his own lights. While he was concerned with leaving the security of a pension, health benefits, a terrific staff, an expense account, and other "perks," this was something he just had to do.

My stomach churned. At forty-something, I had assumed we had finally gotten to the point where, financially at least, things had eased up. For two decades, I had paid my dues by clipping coupons, shopping sales, and taking public transportation. Over the years, I had also prepaid our mortgage, kept a tight rein on our credit cards, and funded our IRAs. Finally, I could treat myself to a manicure without guilt, hire a cleaning service for the heavy household chores, and employ a local teen to maintain the lawn and shovel the snow.

Initially, though it was difficult for me to adjust to these "pleasures," I worked ten-hour days Monday through Friday. And until my forty-second birthday, I continued to work that infamous "second shift" at home. Standing in that fish market, I could see the pleasurable parts of my life begin to evaporate, just like the steam escaping from the enormous pots of chowder.

Then, my eyes traveled to the lobster tanks against the wall. Like the unfortunate inhabitants, I realized I, too, would be imprisoned within my current career as the primary breadwinner. In addition, I would be responsible for carrying the family's health benefits, and I resented my husband for putting me in this position.

The look on my face must have given him an idea of what was going on in my head because he suddenly appeared as a remorseful five-year-old kid. "Oh no, I'm sorry. Forget I even mentioned it," he pleaded. "It was just a stupid dream I had. Just forget it." And he tried to force a smile.

But somehow I knew it wasn't just a stupid dream. It was real. And it was something he had been working up the courage to tell me for quite some time. I looked at him carefully. Somehow I knew the way I handled the next few minutes would impact the rest of our lives forever. I tried a weak smile.

"I've crunched some numbers," he said tentatively, "and while I know that initially, the financial burden will fall to you, I really believe that in one year, I'll recoup my current salary. Then, I'd like you to cut back. Maybe part-time?"

Part-time? I thought, that did sound nice. Before I could respond, the clerk behind the counter was asking me for my order. "The usual right, Mrs. B? Two pounds of flounder and a quart of chowder?"

"No, give us two of your best lobsters, and throw in a dozen shrimp," I smiled. "I have a feeling we're coming into a windfall." And somehow I knew we would.

BARBARA DAVEY

IN THE TWILIGHT ZONE

While traveling in Glasgow, Scotland, I had some time to spare between being dropped off by my bus in the city and the departure of another bus for my next destination. So I walked into Frasers, the most elegant department store downtown for a quick look at the Christmas merchandise.

I entered the store aware that I might not be dressed in appropriate shopping attire. Instead of a chic outfit, I was dressed in khaki pants, waterproof hiking boots, a wrinkled parka, and an indispensable backpack—just like the twenty-three college students I had escorted to Scotland for a fall term of studies. Due to my bulky appendage, it was necessary to maneuver myself carefully between the racks and displays. I saw the quizzical, disapproving looks of the clerks as I walked toward the bright-colored and beautiful fabrics on display.

And then I spotted them: exquisitely patterned silk scarves draped on wooden pegs arranged across the length of a white wall. Scarves are my weakness, and like an addict, I stumbled forward to touch them. As I floated a particularly appealing one across my hand, a tag snagged on my fingers. Hermès it said. *Oh no!* I thought, Hermès, the French company that creates the most expensive accessories available to humankind. So expensive that the tag and every other one I checked were not marred by anything as gauche as a price. What's that old adage? If you have to ask the price, you can't afford it. Undaunted, I was determined not to let my unconventional appearance or the haute couture tag intimidate me into slinking out of this section of the store. I headed toward the closest counter to inquire the price.

Only then did I realize something more than my casual attire was wrong. As I approached the three clerks at the counter, I noticed they were standing in formation, shoulder to shoulder, looking straight ahead. Only the clerk on the right acknowledged my presence, her eyes repeatedly darting my way. I smiled at her; she didn't smile back. Instinct overruled resolve as I gradually changed direction away from the counter and tried to compute this uncharacteristic behavior from a generally friendly and gracious people.

My casual stroll through the department now became a quiet stalk as I searched for an escape into the main aisle. Reaching my goal, I discovered a scene that finally halted my trek. There before me were four people grouped around a display standing motionless, soundless. Human mannequins in street clothes. *What was going on here?* I wondered. Maybe someone was filming a commercial for the store. That's it! There had to be a camera somewhere and these people were posing. Jerking my head, left and right, I looked for any kind of a clue. I didn't see a camera or a video, only more groups of people scattered throughout the store locked in frozen stances as if fired at by a stun gun.

There was no other choice but to surrender to the surreal moment. My own breathing was the largest movement in a world stopped still. So I stood still as a minute passed that seemed like ten.

Then as if by cue, everyone resumed talking and walking. I missed the signal that brought them back to life just as surely as I missed the one that had put them into a trance.

The sudden motion and sound got me thinking. My face colored as I realized what I had done. I had heard the night before on the BBC news that three minutes of silence was to be observed this day, November 11, at twelve noon in the yearly observance of Armistice Day. The entire nation of Great Britain was silently honoring the war heroes of World War I while I was strolling through the store shopping for Hermès scarves. Like a clueless butterfly flitting through a garden of merchandise, I was oblivious to my intrusion on a solemn ritual.

When I told my embarrassing faux pas to one of my students, he said something similar had happened to him the year before. He had spent November 11 in London and had visited Buckingham Palace to observe the changing of the guard. As he was walking down the crowded street, he noticed everyone had suddenly stopped moving and talking. He immediately assumed it was a bomb scare! Propelled by his sense of impending danger, he began running down the middle of the crowded street until the scene around him once again became active with noise and movement. A lady close by asked him, "Why were you running?" Flustered, he told her that he was running to meet a friend and he was late.

Although his response to the situation was the exact opposite of mine, his answer made perfect sense to me. In his panic, I know what his "running to find a friend" was about. Like me, he needed a sign, a reference point, a clue . . . anything to lead him out of three minutes in the Twilight Zone.

MARGO BALLANTYNE

DOING COLLEGE AGAIN—
MY WAY

*T*hree decades have passed since I last went to college. In that time, life has taught me many lessons, and my hair has turned gray. Yet, my idling brain yearned for new experiences and for new knowledge. But while the thought of returning to school stirred my soul, a large part of me held back. How well I remember taking those many required classes and missing the electives that seemed so interesting. I remember the long hours of study and report writing about subjects that seemed so remote to my interests. And I remember the most difficult part of college—registration.

So I struggled about the decision to return to school. For twenty-six years, I lived in a town with a large university. Even before I moved there, I had flipped through the catalog of courses and decided which ones I wanted to take. For reasons that all sound foolish now, I never signed up for any. I put my dream on hold.

Not long ago, I moved to another college town. Another choice point to pursue my dream presented itself. Finally, in a wild burst of determination, I decided to act on my now aging dream and do college my way. This time, unlike my two previous university encounters, I would take elective courses.

With a renewed spirit and armed with the confidence of an experienced adult, I got a copy of the course catalog and reported for the dreaded registration. Oh so quickly I discovered that registering the third time around was not easier simply because I had survived this routine twice before.

Registration at this modest-sized community college was as complicated—and intimidating—as at my previous universities. The process began in the basement of Building E and took me from hallway to hallway, from room to room, and from line to line. It seems that most everyone, except me, was seeking to take classes to fulfill degree requirements. I made it through the first major hurdle—registration—only because of my commitment to experience my dream.

Another challenge now confronted me—where is my class? Knowing my history of getting lost standing still, I decided to find my classroom that day instead of waiting for the first day of school. The room number was clearly marked on my schedule, but where was it? Trying to look casual and self-assured, I wandered up and down the hallways furtively checking door numbers. By the fifth pass, I realized failure lay at hand. For heaven's sake, I couldn't even find my classroom. Was this new experience to be a nightmare or fulfillment of a new dream? I gave up on the classroom search for the moment and let myself be directed to the parking permit office. To my relief, they were very helpful.

Having found the bookstore earlier by mistake, I returned there to treat myself to a brand-new notebook. I ran my hand over the shiny cover and instantly believed its magic promise of the good things I'd store in it. That notebook would open the doors to a whole new world of discovery.

Then another challenge surfaced! I felt self-conscious with being much older than most of the students on campus. The only advantage of age I could claim at the moment was that experience teaches that it pays to come early to allow time for getting lost.

The next week I discovered my classroom, hidden at the back of what seemed to be a big, open office area. Hoping that future tests would be easier than this first one, I walked into my first college class in thirty years. Soon I was rubbing shoulders with teenagers and even another student with (gasp) gray hair.

The class proved to be just what I needed—a shot of adrenaline for my idling brain. We moved through the history of art from cave paintings to the Impressionists. I had taken a somewhat similar course in high school with minimal results. Here was my chance to do it right, and I flew into the assignments, venting years of accumulated enthusiasm into each one.

I admit it wasn't easy to return to the long-forgotten routine of homework, but when a person takes a class by choice instead of mandate, it's a discipline toward pleasure.

Next I tackled a course about Southeastern U.S. history and culture. Because I responded to the professor's nudge into extra-credit projects, I found myself drenched in writing from and about the South. I almost forgot that any other part of the country existed.

Now when I start up the long, peaceful driveway toward the college, I know that shiny notebook has kept its promise. My first experiences with college years ago seemed to focus on what I *had* to do. Now I am doing college my way. I am steeped in those coveted electives—the ones I *want* to take. And life has taught me yet another wonderful lesson—to pursue rather than postpone experiencing my dreams.

BETSY HUMPHREYS

I TEMPED
FOR THE VATICAN

I *was in Rome for a brief visit. Although my Italian* friends were available to get together with me in the evenings for splendid meals, after-dinner espresso and flaming Sambuca with three coffee beans floating on top for good luck, I was alone during the day.

Since I knew Rome, had already "done" the museums, taken in the fountains, and had even tired of shopping for shoes, I decided to contact a temporary employment agency while I was there to see if I could find work that would fill my daytime hours.

When the agency called me at the pensione where I was staying, I was a little reluctant to take the job. They were offering me a few days of secretarial work at the Pontifical North American College Office of the United States Bishops for Papal Ceremonies and Audiences. Bottom line, I would be assisting two Jesuit priests who arranged audiences with the pope for visiting Americans. Having nothing but a wardrobe of micro-mini skirts with me, I wasn't sure if I could get away with this attire in their offices on Via dell'Umiltá in the center of Rome. But I went anyway.

I probably should have been intimidated by the loftiness of the college and the priests and their proximity to the pope, but instead I was just terrified of the telephone that I had been told to answer. At the time, my knowledge of Italian was very limited—at dinner the night before I had just learned the difference between fettucine and fegatini (chicken livers), which I had mistakenly ordered.

Ring, ring. Oh, my God . . . now what do I do? Well, I picked up the very heavy receiver and responded, *"Pronto." Pronto* is the typical response in Italian when answering the phone and it literally translates to "ready" in English. Unfortunately, I wasn't ready for anything.

The operator came on speaking rapidly in Italian, of course, and I could barely get out in English, "Please, please, I do not speak Italian very well." I heard, "Ah, yessah, the signorina Americana, Linda." I was very grateful that she must have already heard that there was an inept temp helping Father Maneiro and she acknowledged me by name. Somehow she managed to communicate with her limited English that she had a very short telex message she needed me to take down and relay to the good priest.

I grabbed a new, long legal pad of paper and a pencil and began to write verbatim. "Ancona, Roma, Roma, Imola, Vicenza, Imola, Napoli, Genoa, spazio, Roma, Otranto, Milano, Empoli, spazio, Torino, Empoli, Napoli, spazio, Ancona, Palermo, Roma, Imola, Livorno. Ancona Zeta 281. Savona, Empoli, Empoli, spazio, Yugoslavia, Otranto, Udine, spazio, Savona, Otranto, Otranto, Napoli. *God help me,* I thought, *how much more of this is there?* Since my printed scrawl was quite large, I had already filled two sheets of the legal pad, and she continued on, "Ancona, Udine, Napoli, Torino, spazio, Roma, Imola, Torino, Ancona. Full-stop. Is okay, Signorina Linda?"

"Sì, sì," I answered lamely. *"Arrivederla.* Goodbye."

I could not imagine what I had just taken down. While I obsessed over the message, I flipped through my three long pages of notes and typed them up so they would at least be readable for the priest. Upon his return, with much trepidation I handed him the typed version, nervously explaining that I had tried to get every word of the message, and profusely apologized for any misspelling.

As he read it, he roared, "Signorina Linda, you did an excellent job, but you know, this message is in English!"

"What?" I asked incredulously.

The operator had spelled out every letter of each word to me using Italian cities (as is their custom)—equivalent to our A as in apple, B as in boy, C as in Charlie, and I had proceeded to take it all down. When I read the telex again I saw that by looking at only the first letter of each word, it read, "Arriving Rome, ten April, AZ 281. See you soon, Aunt Rita."

LINDA H. WATERMAN

In poetry you can leave out everything but the truth.
DEBORAH KEENAN

THE MENTOR

I grew up in a violent, alcoholic family and was left the legacy one might expect when a child is abused, neglected, and given too much responsibility much too early. My spirit was broken, and I was in need of serious repair.

After the painful taking-yourself-apart and putting-yourself-back together task of therapy, I reemerged feeling like a newborn fawn. Though wobbly-legged and unsure of my next steps, I was eager to venture out into the meadow of life. A new beginning, at age forty-six.

I had been writing—a better word would be "scribbling"—my ponderings on paper for years. Spelling and grammatical skills were weak. It was the old days before computers were around to tidy up those pesky mistakes. In spite of my inabilities, I decided to take a ten-day writing workshop taught by a well-known and respected poet.

Feeling awkward and out of place, I sat among thirty experienced poets who discussed each other's presentations with words I'd never heard. I didn't utter a sound. I was the last to present my poem, which was entitled "Out of Focus." I had looked up all the words I wasn't sure of, but I had misspelled the word "focus." My title read, "Out of Focas." The poem was about my father pulling my mother down the hall toward the bathtub to drown her.

The instructor looked at my poem lying on her lap and said to the group, "Focus is misspelled," her tone blunt and unforgiving.

Red-faced, wishing the floor would open up and swallow me, and feeling quite dumb, I stuttered, "I'm . . . a beginner, I . . . I guess I should be in Poetry I instead of Poetry II." Without looking at me and with great drama the instructor said something to the effect that this was *Poetry 96*—emphasizing the "96." I prayed harder for the floor to open, but when it didn't, I took a deep breath and began my poem.

While I was reading I heard gasps and sighs coming from the other students.

It was proof to me that my writing was amateurish, and I had ventured into the wrong meadow. I mumbled my way through the poem, then waited for the ax to fall.

The instructor was silent. The class was silent. I was mortified. After a few moments the instructor picked up my poem, held it to her heart, and said, "God help us all if you are a beginner. This is powerful stuff."

For the next nine days she tucked me under her wing and instructed me on the craft of poetry. She was the ocean; I was a sponge. Between classes, while walking with her or having lunch together, I felt like a schoolgirl whose long socks wouldn't stay up and whose ears stuck out of her Buster Brown haircut.

She told me that I was more than a writer, I was an artist. After asking to see more of my writing, she said that she had shown my poems to other instructors and they, too, had been impressed with my natural skill. She gave me advice about what to read, what workshops to attend, and how to dress when I become a "famous" writer. The things she said were so grand I could hardly comprehend them, but my faith in myself as a writer began to emerge.

In time, a book about my life was published. My mentor—who

went on to win a Pulitzer Prize for Poetry—wrote an endorsement for my book.

I thank God for this woman who saw something in me that I was not yet able to see. Her words reached back through time to help heal, and gave me the courage to venture out into the beautiful meadow of self-discovery.

Shortly after my book was released, I was invited to speak at a large conference on alcoholism sponsored by the Department of Health and Human Services in Washington, D.C. and spearheaded by Betty Ford. I was a guest speaker along with a U.S. senator and the Surgeon-General. Again, I felt out of my league. Sitting on the dais, looking out over a sea of faces, the old feelings of self-doubt threatened to leave me unable to utter a word.

I prayed, not for the floor to swallow me, but for the courage to go on. I recalled my mentor's words about how my poetry reaches into the depths of people. I held on to her faith in me until I could regain my own. I took a deep breath—and a leap of faith—and my words flowed, flawless and sure.

When my presentation was over, a standing ovation told me I had, indeed, touched their souls. Moved beyond words, I stood nodding my head in appreciation. My mentor's gift of validation had led me into a meadow far bigger and brighter than I had dared to dream could exist.

MITZI CHANDLER

MEMORIES AND MODELING

I played the answering machine tape. It didn't occur to me that my mother sounded any different than usual. I glanced at the clock. It was 10 P.M. and obviously too late to return her call that night, so I fast-forwarded over the remaining two messages and crawled up the stairs to my bedroom. My husband was already breathing softly and deeply, as if he had been asleep for hours. I didn't disturb him. I put on my flannel pajamas and gently slipped under the covers.

The phone rang at 11:40 P.M. My husband picked up the receiver by the third ring to find that it was my younger brother Dan. My father had just brought my mother to the military hospital at March Air Force Base. Dan must have relayed the message hurriedly as he was heading out the door. I could hear my husband tell Dan that it would take at least forty-five minutes to get there from Lake Arrowhead, but we'd hurry. "You think it is a heart attack?" was all I could focus on. I ripped off my flannels and pulled on some jeans and a heavy sweatshirt. "Here, Cath, put this on, too." My husband wrapped my heavy woolen coat around my shoulders.

I remember the crunch of the snow under my heavy boots. It was just two weeks before Christmas. My mother's call earlier that evening had been to let me know she had finished the Christmas cards and had mailed them that morning. The car door was stiff with the late night cold. It seemed too heavy to pull open.

"She can stay with us when she gets out," I heard myself saying to my husband. "Dad doesn't have the strength himself to take care of her." The swishing of the windshield wipers caught my attention in the silence that followed. The lights of the oncoming cars seemed unusually bright as they lit the droplets of moisture on the windshield. The side window was cold as I laid my head against it. "She left a message on the machine tonight, but I didn't call her back," I thought aloud.

As we entered the gate of the Air Force base, a feeling of relief swept over me. We were just minutes from being there; to comfort, to support, and to advise. My husband parked as near the Emergency Room doors as the parking situation allowed. The air was now crisp and cool as it often is after a gentle fall shower. The Emergency Room doors glided open. I was blinded by the harshness of the fluorescent lighting and then sickened at the sharpness of the medicinal smell. The air inside was heavy in contrast to the crispness outside.

My family was gathered in a tight circle at the end of the long corridor. The reflection of the bright lights glistened off the well-polished floor. The corridor appeared to lengthen as my brother Dan turned and I saw the look of anguish on his face. My father was seated on a gray vinyl bench that was only one of many that lined the hallway. It looked cold and stiff. He was pale and shaken. My brother moved toward me and I walked on toward him, unaware of the doctor who had come up behind me to usher me in. My husband squeezed my hand and attempted to guide me toward my family. Dan rested his hand on my shoulder and pulled me toward him. "She can stay with us until she gets her strength back," I finally blurted out.

"She has expired," the anonymous doctor whispered behind me. I could hear my father's sobs echoing farther down the hall. The light was blinding and the sounds of the others around me overpowered the moment. Dan lowered me onto one of the vinyl benches and my gaze fell to the floor. I turned my attention to the hospital employees as they made their way in and out of the many rooms down the hall. Doors swooshed open and then closed in a slow mechanical sigh. A young man pushed a laundry cart full of sheets, towels, and hospital gowns down toward the laundry. One of the wheels wobbled and the soles of the young man's shoes brushed softly against the polished floors. I followed his movement as he pushed on down the hall, seemingly an insignificant act. Empty gurneys lined the hall and a cart full of dinner trays sat stoically against the rear wall. The two doors at the farthest point of the hall were labeled "Emergency Room" in large red letters. An "Employees Only" sign was the only thing that kept my brothers and me from entering the confines of the area in which my mother lay.

I could feel a strong hand rubbing my shoulder and I looked over into the face of my husband. "Do you want to go to her?" he asked. Suddenly the lights above me spun and I felt light-headed. Dan pulled at my elbow and signaled me to rise. I couldn't move. My other brothers and my only sister were three feet from me, but they seemed to be at the other end of a tunnel. The sounds of their breathing and the softness of their voices made it impossible for me to respond to them. I'm sure that I sat in that very position for hours, until my husband finally lifted me to my feet. "We'll go over to your dad's with the others." I don't know if I responded or not. Pictures of my mother kept flowing through my mind, and the simple distractions of the immediate environment were the only other items that I could focus on. We walked out of the Emergency Room, through the very doors that only hours ago were the threshold that would lead me to my mother. The sun was coming up, and the crispness of the late evening before had deteriorated to an uncomfortable dankness. I stumbled under the weight of the woolen coat, and beneath the weight of becoming motherless. I was only thirty and not quite ready to be without the guidance and support that I found so often in her.

The drive to my parents' home seemed endless. I didn't want to face the immediateness of her leaving. The hurried manner in which she'd left the house would be painfully obvious. The devastating realization that she wouldn't be coming back would be too much to bear. As I entered the house, I felt a sense of comfort and sorrow that almost swallowed me. So many remembrances of her. Her shoes were casually set next to the door for her morning walk. The lights were still on in her bedroom. The book she was reading sat anticipating her return, marked with a silk ribbon that was frayed from overuse. I couldn't speak. I couldn't express my fears. I suddenly remembered the message on the answering machine at home. I couldn't help but break down in tears. I grabbed the book she had been reading. I clung to it. I wrenched it and twisted it in my hands. I fell back onto her bed and cried. Why hadn't I called her back? Why hadn't she gone to the hospital instead of sitting around addressing cards? Why hadn't I been a better daughter? How could I take back all the times I hurt her? How could I make it up to her now?

A week after my mother's funeral, I attempted to put my life back on track. My husband took me to our Post Office box to gather the mail. Stacks of red and gold and white envelopes fell into my lap. Some of the envelopes contained Christmas cards, others contained condolence cards. One in particular made me gasp. My mother's handwriting was sprawled across the front of the envelope.

As I opened it, I reflected back over the other generous cards and letters that she had given me. She placed one on my pillow for my sixteenth birthday: "Over the years, so much has changed. You're no longer our little girl who needs to be watched over and cared for . . ." She sent another card on my graduation from college: "You are an adult now with your own ideas and your own life to live . . ." She softly placed a tear-streaked letter positioned within a bouquet of white roses on the day of my wedding: "The day of your arrival is still so vivid in my mind and heart. You were a beautiful baby. Thank you for nurturing that beauty from within . . ." Now, the last card or letter I would ever receive from her sat warmly in my hand. I slowly opened the satin-white card with gold lining and read the inscription. "He has delivered unto us this day his greatest gift; his only son." Below the inscription were her delicate turns of the pen that read: "You have been my greatest gift. Happy holidays. May the joy of the holiday season be yours always."

At thirty-eight, I visit the place deep within myself that she returned me to. With each card and letter, I rest there. I promise myself to leave notes in my son's lunchbox, to pin "I love you notes" to my husband's shirts in the morning, and to mail "Thank You" cards in linen envelopes to every person who blesses my life. I return to this place often and continue to strive to be that woman my mother tried to create with each of her simple writings. I strive to be the woman who steadies the world for my family if only for one more day.

CATHERINE VAUGHAN-OBREGON

VI

KIDS ARE
TEACHERS, TOO

I look at the world from a child's point of view.

I'm most comfortable on the ground

looking up.

Jamie Lee Curtis

PRYING EYES

Crash! Waaaaaaaaaaa. "Oh, no! Brian, watch where you're going."

I paused outside the door to the ladies' locker room and listened to the commotion inside. Just a typical afternoon at the YMCA.

Brian, I thought. *How many Brians would be in the locker room today?* Brians in different sizes, answering to different names. Brians from three months of age to . . . well, that was anyone's guess.

I pushed on the door and walked in. Before rounding a pink partition, I read a small sign glued to the wall. MOMS—BOYS AGE SIX AND UP MUST USE MEN'S LOCKER ROOM. "Yeah, how about it, moms," I muttered. *You know who you are. The ones passing off those four-foot, five-inch-tall mutations as six-year-old boys.* I willed my body forward.

Children in different stages of undress ran amok over piles of multicolored clothing. Amid crushed cheese puffs, Cheerios, and Juicy-Juice cartons, sprawled harried mothers coaxing children in or out of clothes. It appeared guppie swim had ended and the barracuda swim group was well into a shark frenzy.

I scanned the room to make sure all Brians were occupied, then slipped off my jeans and pulled on shorts and sneaks. So far so good. I removed my shirt and bra and checked the room again. Just as I suspected. Two draft picks for the Chicago Bulls had me on radar.

"Hi, guys," I said, as I hunched down behind my locker door. "I'm sorry we can't speak longer because if you're not gone in two seconds I'm turning into a flesh-eating virus." They obviously never read *National Enquirer*, for it had no effect.

Some days I'd insert different words to prevent boredom. Some days I ignored them. This time I got lucky and was rescued by a watchful mother.

"Kevin, Rob, come here. Don't bother that nice lady." The woman was wrong. At that moment there wasn't a nice bone in my body.

Not all locker room experiences are negative. A few days ago, an unattached roll of toilet paper slipped from my hands and rolled out the bottom of the bathroom stall.

"Excuse me," I yelled. "Could someone hand me . . ." From my operational command post, I watched as a Brian squirmed underneath the door with the paper clenched in one fist. He beamed with such pride, I hadn't the heart to trash his plastic Power Ranger.

The workout left me feeling calm and restored. And what luck, the locker room had emptied out.

I leisurely removed my sweaty clothes, grabbed my soap and towel, and headed for the baths.

Bang! The pool exit door slammed into the adjoining tile wall and in marched one female "Y" guide, three women, and the McKenzie Elementary School's kindergarten class. As the children looked my way, their pace nearly halted, and they fell upon each other, then rebounded as if from a rubber surface. With deft movements, I hid behind my bouffant shower cap and gold necklace.

I closed my eyes and soaked my hot face under the running water. When I looked again, they were gone—except for one blond boy. His gaze was penetrating; my glare was ugly. His eyes roamed my chest like two supersonic aircraft circling a landing strip.

This is outrageous, I thought. The management must respond to women's dignity, women's decency. On the other hand, this was the most admiration I'd had in years.

"What do you want?" I finally shouted. "Don't you know it's impolite to stare at people? Doesn't your mother teach you manners?" He lifted his finger like E.T. and pointed to my chest.

"Lady," he stammered, "why are you wearing my mom's necklace?"

So much for admiration.

SHELLEY SIGMAN

*I make the most of all that comes, and the
least of all that goes.*
SARA TEASDALE

A WALK BY FAITH

I planted a tulip bulb in the garden today. In fact I planted several of them in the hope that they will brighten my yard next spring when the air is fresh and the rain has washed away the signs of winter. Perhaps they will be red, yellow, or that beautiful shade of purple. I don't know, but I have faith in the fact that spring will come and whatever the colors, they will add a different dimension to my life. That's what the apostle Paul had in mind when he said, "We walk by faith and not by sight." Faith is the leader of all good things to come.

"Hi," said a little girl with light blond curls that hung down over the right side of her face. "You're Doug's mom, aren't you?"

"Yes, I am," I replied as I knelt down to meet the four-year-old's eyes.

"Well, I just wanted to tell you that I really like Doug. He's special."

"I know," I said with a curious voice. "Did Doug talk to you today?"

"No," came the assured, secure answer, "but I like him."

"Me too," I said as I smiled with my face and my heart.

Those are the exact words that were spoken fifteen years ago when I picked my son, Doug, up from his nursery school. They have remained etched in my mind all this time, because I was never ready to write them down until now. Doug is autistic, and he will always be autistic. And yes, the little girl was right, Doug is special.

Doug didn't talk much in nursery school, and he sat in a corner much of the time, always isolating himself from the group. When he did communicate it was with one of the teachers, not with the other students who attended the school. During this time, Doug was also enrolled in a development center for handicapped persons. Our family was on a merry-go-round of emotion, and at one point, it was strongly suggested that we move to St. Louis, where there was a special school for children like Doug. The prognosis was that he'd progress no farther and that he would probably sit and spin objects for the rest of his life. We didn't move. My husband and I were determined that kind of a life was not for us and certainly not for our son. We armed ourselves with courage, knowledge, persistence, and faith.

Doug learned to read while crouched under an easel and listening to Sister Monica at a private school with smaller classes. That lasted only through the first grade because the school suggested that we get Doug special help through the public schools, where funding was available.

In the years that ensued, Doug received speech-language therapy, occupational therapy, physical therapy, private tutoring, various private lessons, special classes in school, and a multitude of group activities like Sunday school, Boy Scouts, karate, soccer, and band. Somewhere between five and six thousand hours of private therapies had begun, but who was counting. We were planting seeds and above all we had faith. Faith that what we were doing was right.

Doug graduated from Chaparral High School, Las Vegas, Nevada, on June 4, 1990, at high noon. He graduated with a class rank of 72 out of 442 with a regular diploma. The week before graduation, Doug received notice that he had been accepted in the learning disabilities program at the University of Nevada Las Vegas. There he will be a drummer with the Star of Nevada Marching Band and as usual, we won't miss a performance.

Life goes on in all of its colors and glory. Each spring we discover a new surprise that perhaps was planted long before and waiting for the right conditions in order to bloom and grow.

Little did the girl at Doug's nursery school know how she had nourished me that morning so long ago as she greeted me with, "I really like Doug."

"I know," was my reply.

Before she left, I asked her, "What is your name?"

She responded melodically while brushing a curl from the right side of her face. "Faith," she said. "It's Faith."

KATHIE HARRINGTON

CANNONBALL!

How could I have known that one hour in the morning and one hour in the late afternoon could create such chaos in my life? Commuting to nearby Savannah for a job I enjoyed had robbed me of "my" time. Even on a well-deserved family vacation, I was a little too tired, a tad too irritable, and always a minute or two late.

"Hurry up, Mom!" my ten-year-old daughter, Meredith, insisted from the side of the pool. "You have to play with me! You promised." She plopped her boogie board into the water and jumped in.

"Okay," I mumbled, "but I'm not sure I remember how." Somehow, deadlines and commitments had replaced my young-at-heart feeling. The last thing I wanted to do was get in the pool.

I caught a whiff of chlorine and dropped the beach paraphernalia on a lounge chair. Already, the midmorning coastal Georgia sun beat down on my head.

"How is it?" I asked.

"It's not too-o-o cold. Come on!"

"In a minute," I stalled, not ready to get my hair wet or to reveal a body with imperfections. I tried to ignore Meredith counting, "One thousand one, one thousand two, one thousand three . . ." and focused instead on the sun-bronzed college students, propped up on white-toweled chairs.

For a moment, I envisioned stretching out on the lounge chair, hiding behind my sunglasses. Of course, no mom is allowed to actually experience this fantasy. We have to *play* in the pool, climbing in and out, traipsing around for everyone to see.

"Mom, are you coming?"

I sighed, sucked in my stomach, and timidly walked barefoot through the crowd of seemingly perfect bodies to the shallow end of the pool. Quickly, I sat down on the top step, plunged both feet into the water, and shrieked, "It's freezing!"

"Jump in." Meredith bobbed up and down in front of me. "It's easier."

"If you splash, I'll get out," I warned her and eased in, feeling the icy rush of water over my arms. "This is too cold," I groaned and tried to avoid a group of kids squealing, splashing, and darting from side to side.

Immediately, I remembered childhood summers spent with friends at the pool, swimming and doing my personal favorite— *Cannonballs! Could I ever feel that carefree again?*

In no time, Meredith scrambled up the side of the pool. "Watch me dive," she called to me. Toes curled over the edge, she raised her arms into position, sprang up and over, slicing through the water in a perfect dive.

"Not a ripple," I said.

Beaming, she swam to my side. Water dripped from her eyelashes, but it couldn't dampen the sparkle in her eyes.

Again and again, she practiced her dive, arcing gracefully through the air as the smooth blue surface rushed up to meet her, and waited for my "thumbs-up."

"Last one," she called to me.

Again, she curled her toes over the edge, jumped up high in the air and . . . hugged her knees against her chest. She hit the water with cannonball force, exploding water in every direction.

"All right!" I clapped my hands together.

In no time, she burst up before me, laughing. "That was so cool! It was like flying. And the whole time I was praying, 'Oh, please don't let my swimsuit scooch up.'" She took a deep breath, then continued, speaking faster and louder with each word, "Then I hit, and the water splashed up, and it came down like rain, and water went up my nose, and—and—." She stopped. Sighed. "It was fantastic . . . Come on, Mom, follow me."

With my eyes open, I slipped underwater with her. Beneath the surface it was cool and quiet, a welcome contrast to the pressures of my normal schedule. Meredith swam an arm's length ahead of me as the sun filtered down through the water. I mimicked her mermaidlike movements and let my body glide with the rhythm. *Ahh,* I thought, *this is heaven. Why didn't I want to get in? Was I so worried about what strangers thought that I'd risk missing this?* Tension flowed out of me like waves depositing discarded shells on the beach.

For the rest of the day, we floated on our backs with our hair fanning out. We dog-paddled, pumping legs and arms up and down in the water, working muscles long forgotten. We hung on to the sides of her boogie board, talking. "A lot has happened," she confided, "that I haven't had time to tell you," and she filled me in on the news. "Isn't this fun?" she asked, finally. Her dark brown eyes held mine, waiting.

I nodded and returned her intense gaze. "What?" I asked.

"You are the most beautiful mom," she said, giving me a fierce hug. "I love you," she added with a tenderness I had almost forgotten.

"You too," I answered, my voice husky.

"This has been the best day!"

Again I nodded, thankful that I hadn't missed it because of a fear of revealing a face with no makeup and a body I presumed to be too old for cannonballs. As I climbed out of the pool, I vowed to adjust my routine to give *playing* its proper due.

DEBRA AYERS BROWN

SOPHIA AND THE
BOOM-BOOM-BOOM

Little Sophia next door had been telling us for the better part of two weeks about the terrible time she had with the boom-boom-boom. She was not quite two years old, and couldn't really talk well yet. However, she had recently progressed from the odd, isolated words she would let fly here and there to complete baby-babble sentences that required close listening to grasp their essence. Perhaps that was the point of her speaking at all. She knew how to get your full attention in a way few orators can—a storyteller in the making.

Sophia and I are friends. She'll climb on me the way my cats do, as comfortable with that as if I were a cushy piece of furniture. She laughs when I tickle her and has recently begun tickling me back. When I go to the park with her and her mother, sometimes Sophia wants me to be the one to catch her at the bottom of the slide, or to help her climb up, unself-consciously offering me a tiny hand to hold. She also likes to come to my place to visit the "mows," my cats, Smokey and Amanda. If she wants to see them while I'm chatting with her mother, she'll steal my keys and make mewing sounds as she walks determinedly out the door and down the hall to my apartment chanting, "Mokey, Mokey, Mokey!"

Late one night, Sophia was jumping around on her parents' bed when she fell off and bumped her head—the incident she referred to forever after as the "boom-boom-boom." Apparently it was a pretty bad boom-boom-boom. I could hear Sophia wailing through the wall and her parents' efforts to console her. But it was late enough that I did not feel welcome to call or knock on their door and ask if assistance was needed. To top it off, there was a confused, non-English-speaking pizza deliveryman in the building, ringing everyone's bell trying to find the correct apartment, and I was attempting to set him straight while also counseling a distraught friend on my static-ridden cordless telephone. So I was not there for Sophia in her hour of need. And it was about an hour before her anguished cries died down.

The following day, I stopped in next door to ask Sophia's mom about the previous night's brouhaha. When I arrived, Sophia was bounding about their living room, apparently none the worse for wear, but she hadn't forgotten about the boom-boom-boom and kept referring to it every few minutes. Babble, babble, babble, babble, boom-boom-boom. She seemed to need to relive the experience, to process it, to understand that a terrible thing had happened, and to figure out why it had to happen to her.

Days later I visited again, and Sophia was still going on about the boom-boom-boom.

"Yes, sweetie, I know," I told Sophia, "I heard all about it. But you're all better now, aren't you?"

Well, sure, but, you know, there was that boom-boom-boom. She told me about it again, and again, and one more time, gesturing dramatically with impassioned pointing in the direction of the accident.

In a watched-over life of playing in the park and Elmo videos and music class, and meals and naps and the love of a wonderful extended family of adoring grandparents, aunts, uncles, cousins, and friends, the boom-boom-boom is a huge event. The catalyst for a sea change, the first inkling that we're not always on secure footing—that life sometimes hurts, and hurts badly.

The story must be told and retold until thoroughly understood, until future safety is assured, until the demons are purged forever.

In that way my little neighbor Sophia is not unlike me, the grown-up teller of tales who lives next door with her two mows. I spend my days writing about my own boom-boom-booms, about the boom-boom-booms that haunt me. The boom-boom-booms of a broken heart, getting older, hard times, and making my way in a world that can be cold, and lonely. Where life—even at its most rewarding and exciting—can be overshadowed by the risk of yet another boom-boom-boom.

Weeks after the boom-boom-boom, Sophia was still talking about it, but the nature of the story changed from disaster epic to cautionary tale. Playing on the bed with great care, Sophia solemnly announced, "No more boom-boom-boom."

I suspect we'll both keep telling our stories, Sophia and I, until we feel all better, until our deepest feelings are known and understood, and we are reassured. That this day will probably come much more quickly for my little friend than it will for me gives me more than a moment's pause.

CAROL L. SKOLNICK

OTHERWISE

I sat eating barbecue next to my brother, Stevie. We were at a picnic given by a group that manages several homes for mentally impaired adults. Stevie lives in one of them with five other men. He has Down syndrome and is considered severely and profoundly retarded.

The pavilion was crowded with people who represented the full spectrum of the degrees of mental impairment. It was not always easy to tell who was an employee of the company and who was a house resident. Nearby, a DJ played music that was being enjoyed by a variety of dancers, some in wheelchairs, others aided by walkers.

Across the table from me sat a very pretty young woman. She was wearing headphones and had several tapes with her, which she switched out occasionally. I noticed she had very nicely manicured nails, delicate features, and just the right amount of makeup. She daintily picked at her fruit salad and when she looked up at me and smiled, I couldn't help but smile back. "I take tiny bites," she said.

"Excuse me?" I asked, wondering if she were speaking to me.

"I take tiny bites," she repeated very slowly so I would understand. She smiled expectantly, waiting for a reply, and so I said, "Well, taking small bites is the proper way to eat." She seemed pleased with my response and continued eating her salad.

When she was finished she introduced me to the people sitting next to her. Then she said, "I'm waiting for my friend. I met him in workshop, and I buy him Sprites. He likes Sprites. He's my boyfriend, and he'll be here, soon."

"That's wonderful," I said. "I bet he appreciates the Sprites."

"He sings to me," she said. "His name is Ricky. Ricky Ricardo." Then she put her headphones back on. Anytime somebody wandered by she repeated the same story. Many of them acted as though they had heard it before.

My heart ached. I looked at the pretty girl across from me with the manicured nails and the perfect smile and wondered what had gone wrong. What had caused this girl to be waiting for Ricky Ricardo to come to the picnic and sing to her so she could buy him Sprites? I could see her, so easily, the way she might have been. I could see her "otherwise." I imagined her laughing with friends, squealing with girls, or holding hands with your average teenage boy.

With my brother it isn't so easy to see what things would be like otherwise. He can't speak and doesn't always seem to be aware of my presence. However, occasionally he will clear his throat or produce a little noise or cough, and I am surprised by the sound of his voice. I can hear in a little gasp of air what it might be like for him to call my name, or laugh out loud, or tease me the way a big brother would otherwise. These moments are disturbing for me but they are rare.

However, this girl with the pretty smile was almost more than I could bear. The otherwise was so painfully obvious that I found my eyes misting over as I watched her. I wondered how her mother, who sat next to her, could bear the constant otherwise. The girl looked up at me and seemed to sense my sadness. As if to reassure me that everything would be all right she said, "Ricky will be here soon." She continued smiling her pretty smile and watching the door.

And then a truly cool thing happened. Ricky showed up. He wasn't quite the Ricky Ricardo I had been thinking of. He didn't have any bongos, and he wasn't in black and white. In contrast to my expectations, he was in living color from his head to his toes. He was wearing a protective helmet and it was covered with bright stickers. He walked straight to us with an unsteady gait.

My new friend received him like a true lady. She looked at me and said, "This is Ricky." I said hello and Ricky said hello and then they stepped out onto the dance floor. They danced and they danced and they danced. She didn't seem to be aware of the fact that he was wearing protective headgear, and he didn't seem to be aware of her otherwise.

As I watched them it occurred to me that the *otherwise* truly doesn't matter. It isn't real. Reality was out there on the dance floor, presenting itself through a kaleidoscope of imperfect, yet joyous, movement. And although quite a few of the dancers were missing the beat they weren't missing the point, which clearly is to take the rhythm you're given, and dance.

CAROL TOKAR PAVLISKA

We're just going to do the best we can, hold our breath and
hope we've set enough money aside for their therapy.
MICHELLE PFEIFFER

YOU JUST HAD TO BE THERE

Not every childhood problem needs a referral to a psychologist, although it may feel that way at times. In fact, there are some problems a therapist could never solve because you just have to be there. Case in point.

Jody, my youngest, had just started kindergarten and things were going remarkably well. I adjusted much better than I expected, and was actually beginning to enjoy the extra freedom it allowed me. Every morning my eight-year old daughter, Lisa, took Jody by the hand and off the two of them would traipse to school. Lisa wasn't always so motherly toward her younger sister, but for the time being, she seemed to be enjoying this nurturing role.

I took advantage of the opportunity one morning to go shopping for the girls. On this trip I bought Lisa a Pokemon card she simply had to have and the winter boots that Jody had nagged me for that tied just like her sister's. Both girls were thrilled, and all was right in the world of childhood. But not for long.

One morning, soon after, Jody woke for school. "I don't feel good, Mommy," she complained. "I have a tummy ache." A mother's dilemma. Such a vague complaint could mean anything.

Do I keep her home from school? Is she just tired? Is there something at school she's avoiding? After a few pointed questions, I decided it didn't sound serious and sent her off to school.

The next morning this scenario repeated itself . . . and the next . . . and the next. She began to resist eating her breakfast, or dallied so long getting dressed that she was running late every day. My frustration grew to anger, and my tongue developed railroad tracks from the number of times I had to bite it.

The kicker came when one morning she refused to wear her lovely new boots, the ones for which she had driven me crazy. "Can I have my old boots back?" she whined. I had already discarded the old worn and tattered boots, but her question drove me to the point of exasperation. I thought Lisa might be able to shed some light on the problem. "Don't know, Mom," she hollered back one day as she ran off to play.

I racked my brain for answers. Was someone teasing her at school? Was the teacher being too strict? Was she not ready for kindergarten and needed to be home with me awhile longer? Was this separation anxiety? After all, not all children are ready to leave the nest at age five. She was just a baby. But the answer came one day in the most unexpected way.

I had had enough. I was going to walk the girls to school and talk with her teacher. As we approached the front steps of the school, the bell rang. All the children, including my two girls, suddenly dashed inside the building as if it were a race to see who could get into their classroom first. In the entrance, I observed all the children quickly slip out of their winter boots and move swiftly down the hall to their respective classrooms. Lisa, like the other children, was out of her boots in an instant and rushing down the hall to her room, leaving Jody struggling to undo the ties on her boots. She didn't see Jody's eyes brimming with tears, looking alone and forlorn as she helplessly watched her sister go.

Like a flash of light, everything came clear! I knew the problem instantly! It wasn't a race to see who could get to the classroom first. It was the fear of being the last one left alone in the hall-way—abandoned. And Jody was it! Day after day! Being three years younger than her sister, she had not yet developed the fine motor skills needed to manipulate the laces on her boots. Other children her age had Velcro or other simple fasteners so they eas-ily slipped out of their boots. These "wonderful" new boots left her behind the pack, alone and afraid to proceed on her own into this huge, cavernous enclave. Her sister couldn't be expected to notice Jody's dilemma. She was busy being a child herself.

How do I know I was right? Because when Jody came home that day I suggested to her that although her new boots were pretty, they seemed hard to get in and out of because of all the ties. Maybe she would prefer to wear a pair of her sister's old boots for a while. Her response—a big smile with an intense hug and a kiss! I could feel her sense of relief. And no more morning problems! No more tummy aches! I wondered how easily such a problem could have been interpreted by all kinds of psychological traumas. How many other problems might fall into this category? Well, for now, all is right once again in the world of childhood. This serious problem had a simple solution. But you just had to be there!

LIBBY SIMON

I am like a little pencil in the hand of a writing God
who is sending a love letter to the world.
MOTHER TERESA

WHAT A WONDERFUL WORLD

I've worked in special education for a number of years. In the beginning, except for the occasional field trip, few special ed children came into contact with children in mainstream classes and although classes were going well, I sensed my preschoolers felt isolated. I never heard them or their parents talk about attending other kids' birthday parties or playing together after school.

One day, on a field trip to McDonald's for lunch, a student and I overheard a young girl asking her mother if she could talk to him about his wheelchair.

"Shhh"—the mother held her finger to her lips and her eyes flicked over to see if we'd heard—"it's not polite to talk about things like that!"

Mother and daughter picked up and moved away.

The boy turned to me and asked, "Why isn't it okay to talk about wheelchairs? It would have been fun to talk to her."

"Some people don't know what they're missing, I guess," I said, looking after the mother and daughter as they pushed through the restaurant doors.

"Maybe," he said, "there'll be a day when people with wheelchairs are just like everybody else."

That evening I talked with my husband, a high school administrator, about the possibility of some of his student leaders performing community service with my class. It turned out that the high school students and staff even raised money for playground equipment. By the year's end, many strong friendships had developed among the teens and preschoolers. I asked the high school if we might publicly offer thanks to the student leaders and were issued an invitation to a year-end awards assembly.

I was worried about bringing a small group of preschoolers, some in wheelchairs, many who could not communicate in any traditional sense, to perform for 1,200 high school students. What could we do that would be well received by everyone, particularly those students seldom exposed to people so visibly different? I thought of the heartfelt way the children sang "What a Wonderful World," the song Louis Armstrong made famous. We ended many days of class with a rousing rendition of the chorus, "And I think to myself, what a wonderful world. Ooooh yeah!" In a way it had become our informal theme song. If we were going to risk performing in front of 1,200 teenagers, I knew this was the song.

I was nervous on assembly day. The audience was silent as several colleagues and I moved the students up on stage with walkers and wheelchairs. I explained that we had come to thank the student leaders for their help and that the preschoolers were going to sing and sign their favorite song. I asked the students to keep in mind that some of the children were unable to sing or even sign in the traditional sense, that they might be nodding or clapping in time to the music instead. I taught the chorus of the song to a hesitant student body, then invited them to sing along when the time came.

I held my breath as the preschoolers began to sing. They started off quietly, but gained momentum with each note. By the end, the entire gym exploded in song and sign and the kids received a standing ovation.

The little boy in the wheelchair who'd previously wished people would see him the way they saw everyone else asked, "Does this mean they like us?"

I smiled and nodded.

"So I can talk about my wheelchair now?"

I'll never forget the pleasure on his face and the faces of the other children as the teens crowded the stage offering congratulations.

Those preschoolers are now in their upper teens and mainstreamed throughout the district. Through the years the memory of our performance has served as a reminder that all people have talent worth sharing. Every year I teach my class to sing and sign, "What a Wonderful World," at school assemblies. With each performance, my students fill me with awe at the capacity of the human spirit to adapt, and I delight in the way in which song and sign can bring people together.

KATHLEEN HILLIARD COYNE

VII
RITES OF PASSAGE

Life isn't a matter of milestones
but of moments.

Rose Fitzgerald Kennedy

CHRISTMAS
MAGIC

The Christmas season blew into the house along with a rush of icy December air. My son's handsome bulk filled the doorway. Behind him followed Melissa, his about-to-be fiancée.

"Okay, let's get this show on the road," he ordered boisterously. "Your timing is on target, Mom. It's cold out there."

He put his arm around Melissa, drawing her close. "It's a tradition." He grinned. "Somehow it's always freezing and windy when Mom decides to go get . . . 'The Perfect Tree.'"

"But, John," I countered, "there's only so much time to get things done before Christmas Eve. The tree has to set in the stand so the branches settle—"

"And if we don't get one today, they'll be all picked over," he finished while ushering us out the door.

We climbed into the car and set out to find the perfect tree. As we drove I realized we were going to search for *my* perfect tree, not *our* perfect tree. Both my children were now independent adults with their own apartments. Even so, I cherished my memories of us as a family searching for the one tree that would symbolize the Christmas spirit in our house.

I leaned forward from the backseat and placed a hand on John's and Melissa's shoulders. "Did you get your tree yet?"

Melissa threw John a darting, sidelong glance.

"No point in it," he replied. "We're leaving for Vermont after we do Melissa's family thing on Christmas Day."

"No tree!" I gasped, dumbfounded, not quite believing any child of mine would forgo a Christmas tree. "But, John . . ."

"It's just not practical, Mom. It'll be dead by the time we get home."

I glanced over at Melissa. She lowered her head, hiding her expression. I sat back in the seat, unsettled. Instinct told me not to pursue the subject any further. *Oh, my! No Christmas tree,* I thought. Somehow, it didn't seem as if a fabulous holiday ski vacation was going to totally obliterate Melissa's disappointment.

Like millions of mothers, I had strived to fill my children's young eyes and hearts with the awe and magic of Christmas. Then later, when they were too old to believe in Santa Claus, I created family events to instill in them the meaning and importance of tradition. I brooded. Where had I gone wrong?

We reached the first tree lot and critically eyed the stock, then left. The perfect tree wasn't there. At the next stop, Melissa seemed to shrink inside herself, offering little comment on two trees John and I had targeted as possibilities. I went off in search of other candidates. Suddenly, I realized I was angry with my son. Couldn't he see how important a tree was to Melissa? Why was he being so insensitive? As I swung around a corner to inspect another row, my questions were answered.

"But, babe, wouldn't you rather spend the money in Vermont?" I overheard John say. "Look at the price of these trees. A hundred bucks, without a stand," he said matter-of-factly, then went on to tick off further items. "No lights. No decorations. Nothing for the top. Come on, babe, wouldn't you like a candlelight dinner looking out at real-live firs and spruces covered with snow? We can enjoy my mom's tree on Christmas Eve and your mom's tree on Christmas Day."

We left the lot empty-handed, but I had a better understanding of the John-Melissa tree dilemma. Their financial status was no secret. John worked part time while attending school and Melissa was just starting her career.

Our next stop was a Christmas tree farm. When Melissa had wandered down a row of stately Scotch pines I took John aside.

"Let me get you a tree," I said.

He shook his head. "No, Mom. It's just not practical. We're going to be gone for two whole weeks. It just isn't a good idea to have a dried-out tree in an empty apartment. Common sense tells you that."

I wanted to take him and shake the living-practical-sense out of his five-eleven frame. Instead, I turned around, pointed to the first tree in my line of sight.

"That's the one. Let's go."

He eyed the overly full tree doubtfully. "You're sure?"

"Yes, I'm sure. Get Melissa." I started toward the bundling stand, muttering under my breath, determined to end Melissa's exposure to my tradition of finding the perfect fragrant, green symbol of holiday spirit.

We dropped Melissa off at their apartment, because she suddenly remembered pressing errands, then continued on home. Later, branches muffled John's voice as he struggled to secure the tree's trunk in our aging stand.

"I know she wants a tree, Mom," he said as if he were reading my thoughts. "But we're not going to be home. I would rather spend the hundred bucks up in Vermont where it really looks like one of those old-fashioned Christmas cards. You know. Snow. Tall trees. An evening sleigh ride. That important ring is going to be put on her finger up in Vermont."

I looked down at my son's face. His expression pleaded for understanding.

"Ahh, I see. Why that's wonderful," I replied gently. "But Melissa doesn't know about the ring, and it won't happen until Christmas. Between now and then I bet she's going to be a little bit unhappy."

I reached down and brushed a lock of hair from his forehead. "Sometimes you have to put practical thinking aside in favor of what's important to someone you love."

His head ducked back under the lower branches. He fiddled some more with the screws in the stand. The tree shook. "Is it straight now?"

I backed away and eyed my plump Douglas fir. "It'll do."

John scooted from beneath the tree's branches, then stood. As he brushed off his shirt and pants he glanced toward the window. "Look! It's snowing!" he exclaimed. Outside, snowflakes were furiously hurtling themselves toward the ground. We watched for long minutes as they blanketed the grass.

"I'd better get going," he said, turning away from the window. "Want me to carry up the Christmas boxes from the basement before I leave?"

I nodded.

Twenty minutes later I kissed him goodbye, reminded him I had extra Christmas decorations, then cautioned him to drive carefully. I made a cup of tea and sat down to gaze at my tree. Its fragrant scent filled the room. I thought about all the Christmas trees I'd decorated in my lifetime. To me each was always perfect. My gaze wandered over some of the collected ornaments I had already carefully unwrapped. Each held within its molecular mass a bit of our family's Christmas spirit. I wanted each of my children to create their own tree-trimming rituals, to combine the traditions of our family with those of the one they loved.

Suddenly, shouts jolted me back to the here and now.

"Mom! Mom!" cried John, as he burst through the door. His words tumbled out in a rush, running into one another. "I was going down Mount Lucas Road—at the turn you'll never guess what happened!"

Oh, my God. He's had an accident! "The car?"

He gave a vigorous shake of his head. "No. No. I was halfway down the road and there it was. A big sign. FREE TREE! I couldn't believe it. I stopped and went up to the house. Somehow they ended up with two trees." He held two fingers in the air for emphasis. "And get this, Mom. They just put out the sign. They weren't in the house more than five minutes before I knocked. When Melissa sees this tree . . . it's fantastic. Perfect shape. Size. Everything!" He threw his arms around me, lifted me from my firm footing, then swung me around while laughing with pure joy.

"I came back . . ."

"For the extra decorations. Now put me down." We held each other at arm's length, our gazes connected by an everlasting mother-child bond.

"Mom, it was like that tree was put there for me," he said. "Like I was supposed to find it and take it home to Melissa."

I touched my son's cheek with its five o'clock shadow. His eyes were bright with the awe and wonder of Christmas.

"It *is* your tree," I murmured, choking back tears. "Yours and Melissa's."

Minutes later he carried a carton packed with lights, tinsel, and an odd assortment of ornaments outside. The song "Oh, Christmas Tree" floated in the air around him, mingling with snowflakes. I watched him go. I knew the young woman he loved was going to be very happy with him—now and for long years to come.

Some may say John came upon the perfect tree by "coincidence." I believe Christmas magic reached out and drew him into its unexplainable mystery and joy.

GERALDINE (GERRY) TRICKLE

Next to beauty is the power of appreciating beauty.
MARGARET FULLER

HER MAJESTY'S MUSCLE

*A*t forty-six, I am in Vanity's gray zone between pride and self-loathing. I have the urge to lie about my age, but then I am truthful, hoping for the "Wow, you look great!" response. One day it became evident that I should forgo that hope and think honestly about getting older.

I am the mother of two sons, twenty and sixteen. I am also a hypochondriac, who often thinks my nocturnal bouts with acid-reflux are, in fact, heart attacks. Having admitted this, you will understand my hysteria when one morning my husband, Len—a physician who does not alarm easily—asked me to lie on the bed so he could examine something. I have not been pregnant for many years, yet there was a protuberant nature to my upper abdomen. "What?" I swallowed hard. In his rushed, early morning "Let me get out of the house" diagnosis, Len said, "It's bulging. Feels like a hernia. I'm calling a plastic surgeon, Dr. Dotoo Much. He knows bellies."

Professional courtesy is not all it's cracked up to be. I got in to see Dr. Dotoo Much that afternoon. Entering his reception area I took a seat in the dimmed light. A romantic glow reflected from the laminated brochures of abdominal surgery. I opened one of the shiny things to read. The outlined diagram in drawing #1 detailed the surgical "correction"—indicating an incision of the entire lower quadrant of the torso. Picture #2 illustrated some major seamwork to put the old girl back together, and the last picture showed postoperative perfection.

A young woman came into the waiting room from behind the locked door and invited me in. After taking a brief history, she opened a drawer and removed something in plastic. "Here," she offered, and handed me a tiny bag that held a pair of disposable panties. I thought for a moment that I was getting a souvenir. I was instructed to change into my new undies and stand in front of the white wall for photos. "The doctor will look at these before he sees you," the young woman said. Then she had me turn to the side so she could get a good shot of my protrusive condition.

When Dr. Dotoo Much appeared in my exam room I was fully draped in a white sheet. We smiled politely, and then he told me to stand in front of him without the sheet. *Okay,* I thought, *this is just another doctor seeing me undressed.* As a certified hypochondriac this happens often. But I'm fairly certain that this disposable panty thing was a first.

A tape measure was stretched up over my torso as the doctor recited numbers in centimeters to the nurse. He asked me to lie down, and he palpated my abdomen in the same manner as my husband had. "The good news is twofold," the doctor announced. "You don't need liposuction [I didn't recall asking for this] but I can fix this condition. It's called rectus diastases."

Decision: I could cry, or wait for him to speak in English. My silence prompted him to continue. "It's from your pregnancies," he said. "You tore the muscle, damaged it so thoroughly, so permanently, that with time and a few extra pounds it forces this bulge." He poked at it. "More or less a herniation." He again pressed into me with his three middle fingers. "But I can fix it," he repeated. "I can make you look twenty again. You could wear a bikini!" Then he added that the corrective procedure is called an abdominoplasty and my unsightliness would take a measly three hours to correct. Luckily, I had done my reading in the waiting room, and I knew what abdominoplasty meant.

"So what you're saying is, you want to cut me open so I can wear a bikini?" I didn't know my voice could get so screechy.

"Look," he said, sitting back on his stool, "I'm an artist. I'm telling you how I see it as an artist." Dr. Dotoo Much hadn't seemed to take into account the travails of a woman who endured the ups and downs of marriage and parenthood long enough to reach the gray zone with this much intact.

At once it crystallized for me—it was time to get out of this gallery. I stood up in my panties and wrapped the sheet around myself. I felt majestic in my robe when I told the doctor I didn't think the surgery was necessary. Rising from his stool, he and nurse I'am Soyoung swung out of the room. I thought I saw a cape trailing behind him.

Then I remembered those pregnancies that ripped my muscles apart. The ones I had taken years' worth of Pergonal to have. Posing in front of the door mirror, gently touching my slight protrusion, I felt a phantom tiny foot still sticking me from under my rib. I smiled, recalling how, together, my husband and I used to feel the baby gently nudging my muscle to find comfort. There was nothing abnormal about my body. In fact, everything was perfectly natural. My pride swelled, and my belly and I adopted a gold medalist's posture, never to be challenged again.

BETH SCHORR JAFFE

THE TIME-TAILORED TABLE

*T*here's a table at the edge of the swimming pool whose occupants I admire each and every day. It isn't where the teen girls sit with their firm, tightly pressed midriffs exposed, striking blond hair over bronze shoulders, smirking at the lifeguard while applying makeup; it's the table of gals just beyond whom I'd *truly* like to emulate.

Their hair isn't silky and wind-swept, and their skin resembles more a map of the majestic Rockies than the smoothness of the bronze blondes'. And rather than tossing their heads in conversation, these gals tend to favor dipping one good ear forward, to hear a friend speak over the din of the nearby pool.

They're the retirees of the pool deck, and I watch them all summer long.

They always choose the same poolside table, these ladies. On crowded days, they apparently arrive predawn to claim it—because by the time I enter at midmorning with my children, all the other tables are filled.

As I observe, these women sit playing hand after hand of gin rummy at a leisurely pace.

Then, when they've finished, they stroll into the pool for a relaxing dip. Next, they pull out a good novel (probably at a specified, prearranged reading time). Pleasurably browsing her book, one of them occasionally glances up, speaking quietly to a companion in the seat beside her.

Their voices are calm . . . their lives are tranquil. They can talk and read when they want to, no questions asked.

They swim at will, with no small hands grabbing at the straps of their bathing suits, demanding attention.

In their sedate state, the ladies have each settled into the swim-suit—(adequate, though not glamorous)—that she will wear the rest of her life. Long past childbearing years, she's finished "spreading," and knows just which bulge or vein needs covering up. There are no surprises, such as the leg band that stayed firmly in place *last* summer, but keeps creeping higher and higher *this* summer, on the hip I thought was still the same size.

Each retiree also wears a nice suntan. It was visible the moment she departed the incoming plane from Tampa, at winter's end. And though too many tans over the years have brought about a certain amount of skin-aging, serenity prevails over any egocentric preoccupation with appearance.

These ladies complete the link between the "teenyboppers" at the skinny, tight-midriff table, and me on my pool chair with the sticky armrests—left behind by the children of the mom who sat there yesterday.

The retirees need never stop reading to answer, "Can I buy another Laffy Taffy, Mommy? I promise I won't drop this one in the pool!"

No one is tugging on their arms asking for more pop or for quarters for the video games inside on this gorgeous, prepaid pool day. Perhaps that's why their arms hang a bit loosely—from the lack of little fingers constantly kneading them. But still, it's a small price to pay.

Do they, I wonder, miss splitting up two fighting siblings (spaced "perfectly" apart age-wise, in order to get along)? Do these women ever long for an ear-splitting voice shrieking, "Mom! There's a bee! Come *quick!*"

Or, as each hits the cool, clear water in ecstasy, is she ever grateful that the siblings are fully grown, independent, and living in St. Louis and Denver?

Obviously, none at the "lady table" apparently needed permission, or a baby-sitter, to come to the pool, all alone, today. What a feeling.

Am I envious of these ladies in their separate, swimming world? Or, do I harbor a small sense of foreboding—wondering what they've done and been through to make it all the way to this mermaidish milestone?

"Slow down," I often tell myself, resisting the urge to tap a textured, sun-soaked shoulder and ask for temporary asylum at their table of solitude.

It's too early, I realize, to adjust to a clean, sticky-free pool chair . . . and quiet reading time. Plus, I decide I'm not quite ready for age spots.

But even with their furrowed tans, skirted bathing suits (and, if you get close enough, a visible varicose vein or two), the occupants of this matriarchal table have surely never sat any prettier—surrounded by peers, and a much-deserved peace.

CINDY KAUFFMAN

The best way to keep children home is to
make the home atmosphere pleasant—and
let the air out of the tires.
DOROTHY PARKER

THE LOFT BED

One Saturday, my son, Devin, and I went shopping for his new bedroom set. He had his heart set on a loft bed he had seen in one of the department store ads, while I had my heart set on a much smaller price tag.

Once in the store, it didn't take long before he spotted the loft bed and sat at its desk. He looked studious with his straight back and folded hands, his feet barely touching the floor.

I could not resist the look of joy on his face as he ran around the bed as if it were his own. He climbed up and down the ladder and opened and closed each and every dresser drawer. So I overlooked the price and purchased the loft bed.

At home I suggested that he put a pencil holder, maybe a picture or two, on the desk. However, a few days later the desktop became just another surface to accumulate things. Broken GI Joes, old greeting cards, candy wrappers, pennies, and crayon shavings now adorned the desktop.

Dirty clothes that did not make it all the way to the hamper sprouted from every dresser drawer, as well as folded baseball cards and signed test papers that belonged in his book bag. The loft bed indeed contained his life as I knew it. It became a disarray of assorted items that at one time had meaning and purpose.

He loved his loft bed. It was his cubbyhole, his own space. His friends also enjoyed this newfound play area. They used it as a military fort, clubhouse, and as the cockpit of the *Memphis Belle* airplane. The extra space underneath also provided room for occasional sleepovers. On the outside, the loft bed was multipurposed and functional. On the inside, my inside, the loft bed still held a boy. My boy.

The boy with four teeth and pudgy cheeks who used to call out, "Up, Mommy" in such a determined voice. The boy who used to kiss me first thing in the morning and last thing at night. The boy who wanted to become a doctor so he could always take care of me and who only needed my presence to once again feel safe and secure.

I remember putting him to bed when he was younger. I would gently tuck the comforter around his body so the cold air or imaginary snakes wouldn't creep in while he was sleeping. Then upon settling down in bed he would become very serious. His deep brown eyes would penetrate through my soul. He would ramble on about his fears, secrets, and dreams. And I would swear as I did most every night that I would keep his secrets *here* as I pointed to my heart. He would then kiss my cheek and drift comfortably into sleep.

As he grew, the nighttime ritual consisted of mostly back rubs or running my fingers through his sandy brown hair, which seemed to retain the smell of crayons and preadolescent sweat. I would recall memories of him. They became his bedtime stories. Each memory became a page in the progression of his life. I would remind him of the times when I slept on the floor beside his bed when a nightmare, lightning, or the death of his goldfish, Belle, had him in a panic. We would laugh at how long he needed to leave the filter running in a tank filled with just water so he could pretend that Belle was still alive. There were still talks about fears, but they were much harder to soothe. His dreams were now more realistic. And the secrets he told me years before, I would swear they were still *here* as I pointed to my heart.

But buying the loft bed halted all these bedtime rituals. The rituals of tucking in, back scratching, and kisses faded as I did if I accompanied him into his room at night. He felt he had grown up enough to put himself to bed. Sometimes he would see me from the corner of his eye and give me a short, obliging peck on the cheek before climbing the ladder to his bed. Most of the time I received a squeaky, "Good night," from high atop the loft bed.

I realized that there would be a fair amount of letting go with or without a loft bed. I knew that this separation would be uncomfortable, for mothers rarely get any preparation for these feelings. The thought of letting go was always off in the distance. I could imagine being happy and proud of how my son had grown into a man. But I also imagined that this future never became any closer.

The loft bed created a separation, an empty painful place. I wanted to have one more kiss, give one more back rub, or lock one more secret deep in my heart.

We moved several years after the purchase of the loft bed. His new room was oddly shaped and could not accommodate the bed, so his loft bed was sold. He reluctantly went back to a traditional twin-size bed and became used to it in time.

Very late one night I thought I heard him calling me. As I walked into his room I noticed something strange and apparent. The streetlight had cast an illuminating shadow across his face. This was not the boy who slept high atop the loft bed. He was different. He was slender and taller. His features were more defined. His comforter was strewn haphazardly around his body. Tears welled in my eyes. He hadn't called me. He was fast asleep. I walked toward his bed and ran my fingers through his sandy brown hair, which had lost the smell of crayons and preadolescent sweat. I leaned over, kissed him lightly on his cheek, and whispered, "I love you."

And as I straightened up to walk out of his room, I heard him murmur, "I love you too, Mommy."

I took a long look around his room before leaving. The junk that had occupied so much space before was gone. It was replaced with items he had acquired on his own. The top of his dresser held a watch, a model of a car, and a wooden box with a sign that read, KEEP OUT. And I realized that I no longer held the layout to his room. Tears welled in my eyes once more, not for what I lost but for what I was about to gain. A beautiful young man who was becoming independent, but who would always be my son.

He may never again tell me his fears or dreams. But I still have the memories and the secrets locked away in my heart.

MOLLY MEYERS

LIBERTY'S
TIMELESS GLORY

lmost *fifty years have passed since that momentous journey*, and my first glimpse of that lady with the torch, but the memory is still vivid in my mind.

I boarded the old Navy ship as a fourteen-year-old girl haunted by her past. The *General M. B. Stewart* was in the port of Bremen, Germany, and I was with my grandparents (who raised me) and hundreds of other immigrants lucky enough to be going to America on that September day in 1951. The saying in the refugee camp where we had been living was that "in America, the streets are paved with gold." We knew that it was not actual gold, but golden opportunities for all who lived there.

Once we were aboard ship, women and children were ushered to one area, men and older boys to another. Then we were assigned sleeping bunks. I got the upper bunk, Grandma the lower. Grandpa, of course, went with the men. After settling in with our meager belongings, Grandma and I went up on deck, where Grandpa was already waiting for us.

As the ship pulled out, someone burst into the song *"Auf Wiedersehn"* ("Till We Meet Again"). The song brought tears to the eyes of many passengers. I remember studying my grandparents' faces; their eyes revealed the bittersweet feeling I shared. We all knew we would never see our old homeland, Hungary, again. World War II had changed our lives forever, making us displaced persons, refugees. But we were on our way to America now, the land of golden opportunities!

Our Atlantic crossing took ten days, most in stormy seas. My grandparents were seasick much of the time, but I thrived and even made some new friends. A young American, Dave, who worked in the ship's kitchen, brought me my first Coke, a new taste delight, and asked where I was going in America.

"I go to India," I had told him in my best English, which I had studied for two years at the refugee camp.

He smiled and said, "That's probably Indiana, not India. In-di-a-na," he emphasized, adding, "You will like it in America."

Most of the kids on ship whiled away the hours playing games and watching Roy Rogers movies in the ship's enormous game room. But excitement was easy to find, too. One day, while a friend and I shared an easy chair, huge waves hit the ship, throwing the chair across the room and sending everyone in its path scrambling for safety.

In the equally enormous mess hall, where we went for our meals, we often had to hold on to our trays with one hand to keep them from sliding off the table. On deck, we frequently watched porpoises at play in the water. One day we saw another ship. It turned out to be the *Queen Elizabeth*. And when we chugged past the white cliffs of Dover, we sang, "There'll be blue birds over the white cliffs of Dover" in their honor. Someone in the game room had taught us the song.

Then one morning before dawn, Grandma woke me.

"Get dressed, honey. Let's go up on deck. I hear the lights of New York are visible in the distance!"

Once outside, I remember gazing sleepily into the black distance, becoming entranced by the trillions of lights out there on the dark horizon. It looked like a fairyland. Those were the lights of America!

As dawn broke, someone shouted, "There she is! There she is! The Statue of Liberty!"

I stared, mesmerized, on the vision of the lady with the torch—magnificently rising out of the sea. From my vantage point on the ship, she seemed to hold her torch higher and higher on the sky-line.

I recall being so overcome with emotion that it seemed I could actually hear her speak the famous words I had learned in English class, "Give me your tired, your poor, your huddled masses yearning to breathe free." So that moment in time became indelibly etched in my memory. It was the most thrilling moment of my young life!

Later, as we all streamed off the ship, I was compelled to look back at Miss Liberty's glory one more time. But it was not until a few years later that I came to understand what she truly stands for.

Almost fifty years later, I took a trip to New York City with my ten-year-old granddaughter, Nichole, and we went to see the Statue of Liberty. She is, after all, one of the most famous icons of this great land.

After we passed through Castle Clinton, along with hundreds of other people, we found ourselves at the water's edge. Then we boarded the three-level ferry, and sat on a bench. I took a deep breath. For as we left Manhattan, facing us in the opposite direction was the famous lady with the torch. Memories of my first sight of her flooded my mind, and tears welled up in my eyes. A woman sitting on one side of me handed me a tissue, and smiled at me.

"I first saw her years ago, too," she said. "I know how you feel."

My granddaughter would have liked to climb the steps to the top, but agreed that the elevator would be easier on me. The elevator took us to the top of the pedestal, where we peered out the windows at the top of Miss Liberty's ten-foot-wide head. The 180-degree view was fabulous.

"See, way out there on the Atlantic Ocean is where I first saw Miss Liberty from," I told Nichole, pointing out to sea.

"You were very lucky that you could come here, weren't you, Nana?" Nichole asked earnestly, seeing me wiping away the tears.

"Yes, I was very lucky, and you are even luckier, because you were born right here," I told her, as we turned to leave.

Then suddenly, I saw a vision of a ship out there on the open sea, carrying hundreds of those tired and poor, "those huddled masses yearning to breathe free." I waved to them and whispered, "You have found a wonderful new home."

RENIE SZILAK BURGHARDT

MOOPY
AND THE RANGER

My son is outside in the garage asleep in the back of his new Ford Ranger. He has his portable phone with him, his alarm clock for school tomorrow, a can of Dr Pepper, and Moopy, his stuffed Snoopy he's had since he was a baby.

He wanted the truck, but he didn't know we were really getting it for him. I kept telling him there was no way we'd be able to afford it.

"Forget it," I said. "You're going to be using our cars when we're not using them. End of conversation."

But I know he saw the catalogs we brought home and forgot to hide, and when the dealer called to say the truck was in, he forgot that the truck was a surprise, and left the message with my son: "Tell your mom and dad the truck is in." The car dealer said he covered his steps and said, "The truck your dad was looking at for himself," but my son is smart . . . too smart.

My son is using his savings from good report cards, birthday money, and taking care of our neighbor's yard during the summer to pay for the deposit. We told him this arrangement after he saw the truck; there was no argument. My husband and I decided this would put some of the responsibility of ownership into our son. Seeing my son asleep in the back of his new truck, I don't think a penny of his savings will be missed. We're going to pay the monthlies as long as he does his job and gets good grades. He is going to pay for gas with his summer job. If he's out of money, he just won't be able to use the truck. He's also paying for the insurance. I think this is fair! With privileges come responsibility in the real world.

Today was my husband's day off. We picked up the truck early, and he drove it home.

"He's just gonna love it," my husband said as he got out. "It handles comfortably and has just enough pickup for a safe first vehicle."

Our neighbors all saw my husband pull into our driveway. A few came over to ask, and we told them it was for our kid and that he didn't know about it. I was very proud when one of them said, "He's such a good kid. If anyone deserves it, it's him. He's going to love it."

We pulled the truck into the garage so it wouldn't be seen from the street. We just listened because he comes in through the garage.

I can't write down the sounds he made. But I've never heard him so excited. We ran out to see him as soon as we heard him whooping and hollering.

"You got me a truck! It is mine, right? Wow. This is so cool. Wow. So totally cool. And it's red. I wanted red. Oh wow. I can't wait to call Crystal. Oh wow. I can't wait to call Brian. You guys are great." His smile was all teeth and very genuine. And then the magic words, "I love you guys."

He went outside an hour ago to go to sleep in the truck. We watched—and laughed when we saw that he was bringing Moopy, his stuffed Snoopy, his favorite stuffed animal from when my baby was a baby.

"So, why are you taking Moopy?" I asked.

"I share everything with Moopy. Where I go, Moopy goes."

Then he took Moopy and said to him, "Tomorrow, Moopy,

we're going to go out in our truck and meet some women . . .
after we dust it."

FELICE R. PRAGER

I'm cherishing what is left vs. mourning what is lost.
AUTHOR UNKNOWN

AUTUMN LEAVES

There I was, merrily bouncing along living my life with gusto, when the seventh decade slammed into my face. Totally unexpected, you understand. I mean, I knew it was coming, but I wasn't prepared at all. How does one do that, prepare to be sixty years old, when you feel like Peter Pan and still experience the joy and fairy-dust exuberance of youth?

The birthday came and went with the usual party, cake, and funny cards and no particular angst on my part. It was later, a few days—maybe a week or so. The ever-popular leaf season had arrived, a time when I traditionally spend hours outside, raking and lugging leaves to create a mulch pile worthy of Mr. Bunyan.

After just three hours, realization hit—my yard-marathon days were over. Bones creaked, feet ached, and the back of my neck hurt like crazy. Defeated, I crawled into the house and prepared to take a nice, long shower. I could give a long dissertation on what I saw in the mirror, but some of you already know that story. Wrinkles, lines, sags, and bulges: all were mine. That was no strange woman staring back. Just me in all my aging glory. Yeah, yeah, I've heard all the yarns about old wood, wine, and books being the best. But did you ever notice old wood becomes pockmarked with termites, aged wine bottoms out with thick sediment, and antique books crack easily and cast a sick, yellow glow? All quite un-becoming, I'd say. This was a major depression here, something I surely had not counted on.

Strolling through the shops, I began looking for skin creams and oils at the Lost Youth counters. I wondered if I was gray yet—I'd colored my hair for so many years, that I had no clue. Perhaps, if I left off with the dye and let myself be gray, fewer demands would be made on my poor old self. I wandered the shopping mall to buy nothing, just searching for I knew not what. I roamed through my house—dusty like me, and made mental lists of who will inherit what from my largesse of knickknacks and clutter. I thought about cooking more. After all, that's what old women do—cook, while the old men putter. It's easier than doing nothing.

I imagined a stranger browsing over the obituary page. He sees my name, reads my age, and fleetingly thinks, "Ah well, she was here long enough anyway," and his eye rushes ahead to read the next name, searching for someone young so he can mourn for a moment.

Reading the newspaper, I notice an announcement, "Free Flu Shots Tomorrow at the Senior Center." I take my husband with me. We'd never been to the Senior Center before. It's a lovely building with parklike grounds and very young workers. "I never thought it would come to this," I mutter.

We arrive early and begin to form a line against the wall. I am number twenty. Carefully, I watch as people assemble in the hall. Such an assortment of folks to examine. Some in walkers, some bent far over as though looking for a pin dropped on the floor. A few strut smartly, determined to show their vigor, while others shuffle along in their white athletic shoes. The dress code is eclec-tic: outmoded polyester slacks and sweat suits in bright, gay col-ors. Some outfits look very bedraggled and worn and one sprightly old fellow sports a Tommy Hilfiger shirt.

In comes Aunt Eunice, owner of the famous Eunice's Restau-rant. She turned eighty last year—one year after some thugs beat her up and left her for dead on the city street. Our local television station did a whole series on her, as did the newspaper. Everyone rooted and prayed for her and she made it through the ordeal just fine, bringing home bags and bags of cards and gifts from strangers and friends. She still goes to work every day to bake biscuits and ham for her patrons.

Aunt Eunice wears a great grin on her face and orthopedic sandals on her twisted, bandaged feet. She is our poster person for the State Arthritis Foundation and now I see why. The big toe on each foot turns at complete right angles. How in the world can she smile with such painful feet? I admire that in a person.

Sitting on a bench across from me are two very old people. Together they weigh less than I, but their smiles are much bigger. Regally they sit, greeting all comers with handshakes and niceties. The lady does the speaking, "So very nice to see you again." Unconsciously, her arm reaches out from time to time to pat the husband's frail back.

Over by the door to the auditorium, where the shots will be administered, a man sits in a chair, laughing and loudly directing folks which way to go. He looks to be a bit older than I am and soon it's apparent that he is the son of the aged couple on the bench. He darts over each time someone comes to greet his parents to remind them just whom they are greeting.

Everyone in the room is cheery, and no one grumbles about the long wait. I wish I were sitting on a chair so I could offer it to Aunt Eunice. It must be hard for some to stand so long.

Finally, we file into the big room and sit to await our number. I am seated just behind the little man and woman and their cheerful son. What a happy, happy fellow he is. Proudly, he tells us, "Pop is ninety-one and Mama just turned eighty-six." He helps his father off with his jacket and four sets of hands, mine included, reach out to help his mother.

I am glad to see the deference shown by the old to the older. There is something here I want, something I can look forward to.

The young volunteer nurses seem to enjoy themselves. Everyone is laughing and smiling and no one is in much of a hurry. This is leisure. This is life in the autumn years. Thanks to a little visit at the Senior Center, depression falls away like autumn leaves and I no longer fear my December.

LYNNE LAYTON ZIELINSKI

THESE BOOTS WERE MADE FOR WALKIN'

While on an extended trip to England after I graduated from college, I once again found myself standing at my closet feeling helpless as I looked at my wardrobe. The plain white T-shirts and baggy khakis of my school days hung dull and lifeless. The shirts weren't exactly white anymore; they were closer to the typical pale gray that is the backdrop of the British Isles. As for my feet, I had only packed my well-seasoned tennis shoes, and in London, you might as well use the American flag as a shawl if you wear tennis shoes any place but a tennis court. Those shoes seemed to scream, "Yes, I am a tourist and no, I don't have a lick of fashion sense."

People would regularly stop me in the tube station to ask if I needed directions. For the most part, I knew where I was going, but I did feel just a little bit lost. I started to notice that in my old slouchy clothes, I slouched too. I used them as a way to hide my womanly figure, because I thought I was fat. I thought I was supposed to be skinny and boyish-looking, like all those skeletons in the fashion magazines. I wore boring styles and drab colors because I didn't want to stand out in a crowd and risk people pointing and laughing at me the way they did at high school dances. I had developed faster than most of the girls in my class, but instead of feeling good about becoming a woman, I was given nicknames that I didn't even understand. Yet, I definitely knew they weren't compliments.

In college, I finally started to receive some compliments about the way I looked. But I still wasn't comfortable with my figure. I felt that my breasts were too big, and that I wasn't supposed to have hips of any kind. Darn those magazines! But I believed them, and so I continued to hide myself in my clothes.

But on that gloomy day in London, I decided I had had enough. I wanted to feel as sophisticated and confident as the women I saw walking up and down Oxford Street. So I did what any self-respecting woman does when she's feeling a little low. I went shopping.

"All I want is a little pizzazz," I told the sales associate at Marks & Spencer. She brought out a short black skirt and a bright red sweater.

"Go on, just try them," she said, as I protested that the skirt was too short for the kind of legs we were dealing with. "You Americans," she laughed, "You're always so hung up about your bodies."

I came out of the dressing room and when I looked into the three-way mirror, I wasn't quite sure that all of those reflections were really mine. My legs hadn't seen the light of day for ages, and I definitely wasn't used to wearing a sweater that couldn't double as a tent in a pinch. But as I got more and more used to that image in the mirror, I began to think that it wasn't so bad. I realized that by wearing clothes that were several sizes too big for me, I actually looked bigger than I really was. Worst of all, the weight of that extra fabric didn't just weigh heavy on my body, it weighed heavy on my soul. No, I was not skinny and shaped like an adolescent. I still didn't look anything like the fashion magazine waif. I was, however, shaped like a woman, strong and healthy, and that was exactly as I should be.

I bought the outfit, of course, not to mention some other better-fitting pieces. But I needed one more thing: something to replace those old dingy tennis shoes.

I walked over to the shoe department and spotted a gorgeous pair of sleek black boots. *Far too sophisticated for me,* I thought. But then I thought again. I slipped them on and once again looked in the mirror.

"Verrry smart!" I heard the British accent from behind me. I assumed it was another associate who was just trying to make a sale, but I turned around to find a fellow shopper.

"They were made for you," the gentleman said with a sincere smile as he walked out the door.

He was absolutely right. And as I walked down Oxford Street in my comfortable new ensemble, a young couple stopped me and said, "Excuse us, miss, but could you tell us how to get to Victoria Station?"

AMY LYNNE JOHNSON

VIII
A PARADIGM SHIFT

Every time I close the door on reality

it comes in through the windows.

Jennifer Unlimited

MY LIFE

When you have children, you do things you never thought you would do. Your life changes in ways you can't even imagine. And you have days so strange, so chaotic and unpredictable, that you know you could not pass a psychological evaluation if your life depended on it.

This was one of those days. The morning had gone badly, but it wasn't until after lunch that I realized with a sinking feeling that it wasn't going to get any better.

"Mother," Tori shrieks, "Sophia's pinching me!" Massaging my temples, I march into the family room.

"Uh-uh! Uh-uh!" Sophia chants, denying her guilt. Her pudgy, toddler hands are filled with the flesh of her big sister's thigh. I rescue my four-year-old, and quiet her sobs with kisses and hugs. Sophia is jealous, and in response to her shrill voice, my heart begins beating at breakneck speed.

"Let's paint with watercolors," I coo, praying they agree. The girls scramble to the table, and I hand them their brushes, which they use as drumsticks while I gather the paper, two cups of water, two paint boxes, two stacks of napkins. I roll out the newsprint paper (large enough to cover the table—so they won't run out of space too soon).

Satisfied, I turn the corner into the kitchen. The day's dishes line the sink. The dishwasher needs unloading. Yesterday's mail is heaped on one end of the counter; my notebooks and Daytimer clutter the other. There are bills to be paid . . . but first, I have to wash these dishes.

Almost finished, I realize that the girls have been quiet for at least five minutes. *Ah . . . the magic of Art.* The words "Mother of the Year" streak through my mind like skywriting on a clear summer day. I peek around the corner, hoping to catch my darling Picassos at work.

They are covered in paint. Hands, arms, faces, clothes—saturated. Tori watches in eerie fascination as her sister stuffs the paintbrush into her mouth.

"No, No, No!" I wail. "Paint belongs on *paper,* not on bodies!" Suddenly, I think of the forgotten Valentine's gift I gave to my husband a few years back: Glow-in-the-Dark Body Paint for Lovers. I wonder if it is still lying unopened in our closet somewhere. Hmmm.

I shake the thought from my head. "Bath time," I announce, in the tone of voice you might expect if I had said, *"Time to go to the circus!"*

Upstairs, I pull shirts over protesting heads and pants off unwilling feet, then hurry the girls into the warm water. Half a bottle of Baby Magic is required to render their skin tone pinkish and the bathwater a sickly brown. Suddenly, an insistent knock sounds at the front door. Someone rattles the doorknob. Alarmed, I order my daughters to stay put. "I'll be *right back,"* I tell them. Then I hurry down the stairs.

Brittanie, my ten-year-old, peers through the window. *Home from school already?* I have lost track of the time.

"Mom," Brittanie whispers when I swing the door open. "What's wrong?"

"Tough day, honey," I answer simply, closing the door behind her. Just then, I hear the unmistakable sound of four wet feet on the floor. Two at a time, I take the stairs, rushing to circumvent the tragedy about to unfold. Too late. Wet feet slip on the vinyl. Two round bottoms hit the deck with one loud *thud.* Screaming erupts. Brown water now covers the bathroom floor.

Toweling off the girls, I reflect on my own childhood. Fear of bodily harm would have kept me in that tub at my mother's command. "Heads will roll!" she often thundered, as one possible consequence to disobedience. I lived in fear of the image that evoked—and of the sharp sting of a slap on the bottom, or a knuckle rap to the skull.

But pain is not a consequence we parents are encouraged to employ these days. Logical explanations. Diversion tactics. Time-outs. These are acceptable—but lately none of them work for me. I look longingly at the hairbrush on the counter. *One small whack each?* My hand inches forward. *No.* I put the hairbrush in the drawer.

"Now it is time to get dressed," I say firmly, impressed by my display of self-control. Sophia squirms. Wiggles. Wins the battle . . . and runs joyfully down the hallway to her room.

"Naked, naked, naked," she sings, arms waving wildly above her head. The light loves her supple, pale skin. Her chubby thighs and buns jiggle as she runs. I watch, entranced by the beauty of her.

Reluctantly, I turn back to the bathroom, where I drain and rinse the tub. After drying the floor, I gather the dirty clothes and then stop cold at the noise of fighting in the bedroom. Clothes and towels hit the floor.

"One moment!" I scream, standing in the doorway. "Can't I have just *one moment of peace?*" From a corner of the bedroom, six brown eyes study my face. A fleeting sense of victory lifts my spirits. Then, Sophia whimpers as a yellow snake slithers down her legs and coils on the carpet. "Pee-pee! Pee-pee!" she cries, pitifully.

This time, the diaper goes on easily.

"You're scaring us, Mom," Brittanie says to the insane, hysterical laughter escaping my mouth. Ignoring her, I dab furiously at the carpet with a damp cloth. "Is this my life?" I ask the ceiling,

"This can't be my life!" High up in a corner, way out of reach of my swinging towel, a dirty cobweb waves mockingly.

My daughters and I spend the rest of the day huddled over bowls of popcorn, watching videos—something I swore I'd never do, before I actually had children.

Later, when my husband comes home, I step out of the house for the first time all day. I get into my car. Numbly, I drive up and down quiet streets contemplating the lighted windows of the homes I see, wondering about the occupants. I stay out until I am sure the kids are in bed.

Back home, I sneak upstairs. I am not even *tempted* to gaze at the angelic, sleeping faces of my kids. Tiptoeing past their room into my bathroom, I undress in the soft light shining through the window. Looking at myself in the mirror, I think of Sophia running down the hallway and the way her skin glowed like a pastel moon.

Time has touched my body with its unforgiving heavy hand. Motherhood, too, has left its mark; my thighs, stomach, breasts bear the subtle silvery streaks I remember on my mother's skin, but never imagined on my own. Lifting my arms above my head, I pause and wonder if *I* ever ran wildly, with naked abandon. I don't remember how that feels. Sighing, I pull my nightgown over my head. While brushing my teeth, I think of the comfort I'll find next to my sleeping husband. Quietly, I crawl into bed.

But something is wrong. I sit up and look over at Michael. He is clinging to his side of the bed, driven to the edge by two sleeping bodies. Two blond heads have stolen his pillow. Exhaling loudly, I collapse on my pillow and pull the comforter up to my neck. Tori's cold feet seek warmth; I snuggle them between my calves.

Michael's slow snores and the soft cooing sounds of sleeping children combine to make music worthy of a queen. Listening, I feel a contented smile spread across my face, melting the tension.

Out in the darkness, a dog barks and the coyotes call across the meadow, from the hill that is their oasis.

"This is my life," I whisper, just before sliding into a deep dreamless sleep.

LUCI N. FULLER

DEMOCRAT CAKE

*I*f Charlene knew the governor's wife took her cake home, she'd absolutely die on the spot, and that's no lie. She's an expert when it comes to baking. Why, she's taken the blue ribbon at the Home Extension plenty of times, but the governor's wife is another story. She's a Republican, but to Charlene, that's being the devil himself, or worse.

I wound up with Charlene's cake at the VFW meeting last Thursday. As usual, Charlene and a couple of others had made desserts to raffle off, and the next thing I knew, I had a whole cake on my hands—a good one, too, with the real shredded Hershey bars and genuine cocoa. Charlene doesn't skimp on anything and that's the problem. I know a decent dessert when I see one. Lord, you only need to look at my thighs and know that!

Well, it wasn't twenty-four hours until I got a call from Retha Fuller asking me to the Republican Ladies fundraiser. Now, I've been a member for years, but I probably wouldn't go if Retha didn't goad me each time. They're a nice enough bunch, but I don't have much in common with Sunday golfers and Episcopalians. Too much money and not enough Bible if you ask me, but I'm not one to say anything.

"Governor Stewart is going to be here, and I really like Phyllis," she said.

I blinked hard. Of course Retha and the state's First Lady couldn't be on a first-name basis, but I went along with it. When Retha said there was going to be a cake raffle, a light went on in my head. I could dispose of Charlene's cake with the Republicans!

So what if one of Polk County's hottest Democrats baked it? Nobody would need to know, and I wasn't about to tell them. I said I'd bring a Hershey Bar Cake right on the spot.

I met Retha at the door that night with the cake in tow. I'd been asked to write up a little something to go with it, which set me to wondering if anybody would ask for a recipe, so I decided I'd have to fudge. I wrote, "Hershey Bar Cake. America's chocolate bar and a dieter's downfall" and hoped for the best. If anybody asked, I'd just say it was a secret. That wouldn't be a lie.

Several of the women oohed and ahhed at that cake sitting there next to a Coconut Orange and a genuine Lady Baltimore. All of them looked real good, but I didn't give in to temptation. I knew better than to try to bring any home. I didn't need the first one, and I sure couldn't afford the second one even though it would be for a good cause.

Retha made it a point to introduce me to Phyllis Stewart, who was seated at the head table. She was more attractive than her pictures, there in that pale blue suit and corsage. She smiled and nodded, and called my friend "Retha" only after she'd glanced at her name tag. That was a dead giveaway, but Retha kept going on about the last time they'd met, like they were bosom buddies. Of course she would help Governor Stewart in the campaign, of course the Stewarts would be coming back to Polk County, and of course they would be sure to drop by the annual fish fry. I suppose Retha would be gabbing with her yet if the county chairman hadn't rapped the lectern.

Well, we took our seats and heard a few talks and silly carryings-on about the Democrats in the state legislature. Then Mrs. Stewart got up to say that her husband would veto any bill for a state lottery.

"It won't happen on our watch, that I can assure you," she said. "Other states may say gambling will cure our ills, help education, and turn our budget around, but don't you believe it! The lottery plays on the poor man's vice. It sells false hopes and dreams to people who can least afford it!"

Everyone applauded, though I knew there were plenty in that room who played video poker down at the 7-Eleven and bought tickets across the state line. Why, Retha had even admitted to doing that, but I kept quiet.

There we were, ready for the cake raffle. The chairman was acting auctioneer, and I could tell he'd done this before.

"Fifty? Do I hear fifty to start?"

I couldn't imagine paying fifty dollars for a cake plate, much less a cake, but sure enough, the rich golfers in the crowd commenced to bidding.

"O.K, I have a bid for a hundred dollars. Do I hear a hundred-fifty?"

Nobody budged.

"A hundred-fifty? Come on, folks! It's made from real Hershey bars!"

Hands shot up and before that sale was through, Charlene's Democrat cake had sold for a full 225 dollars. I couldn't believe my ears when he announced the high bidder was Phyllis Stewart!

Visions of Charlene swirled through my head. Why, if she knew her cake would bring 225 Republican dollars and it was going home to the governor's mansion, she would have put Ex-Lax in the recipe, sure enough.

Now I suppose Governor Stewart has eaten Democrat cake before. Everybody knows there aren't enough Republicans in this state to elect a governor on their own, but I never did tell Retha whose cake it really was. She'd die on the spot if she knew I'd brought contraband to the Republican Ladies. Why, that would be like serving road kill for Sunday dinner!

So I'm keeping my lips sealed. What they don't know can't hurt them.

TAMMY WILSON

*If you can't pronounce an ingredient on a label,
it's a good idea not to eat it.*
ELEANOR GOODMAN

MARTHA STEWART
IN DISGUISE

ive years ago, my children grown and my husband's business doing well, I quit my job. I decided it was time to do some of those things I had always planned to do when the kids were grown, when I had some extra cash, when I had some extra time . . .

My first Monday off work, I got up out of bed, looked out the window, and said, "Now I'll have time to smell the flowers." My words brought me up short. I took another look out the window. There were no flowers. In fact, there wasn't much besides some tired bushes and a weedy, if mowed, lawn. I shrugged. Oh well. I had never been much for the outdoors. For me, the yard had never been anything more than a buffer to keep us from living right on the road. A place to chase the kids to when they were little. "Smelling the flowers" was, after all, just a figure of speech.

That morning, my yard consisted of the north side where the overall theme was insect life forms, the south and west sides, with brown as the unifying color, and the east side, which faces the road. The east side was kept clipped and mowed, not for beauty but for neatness, much like my toenails.

That was five years ago. It all started with some vegetable plants. Ever practical, I decided that with such a large yard and so much newfound extra time, it would be fun, profitable, and soul satisfying to plant something I could bring to the table like Lady Bountiful. I read up on gardening, learning about bugs, cultivation, and fertilizing. I turned the television on, and Martha Stewart and I began planning how I was going to fill my pantry and my freezer. I envisioned myself out there in the dewy morning with Martha, wearing my wide-brimmed hat and my gloves (the way we used to dress for Easter, actually), carrying a vintage basket and clippers, harvesting the day's supper.

That was the vision. The reality was, alas, less romantic. First of all, there is no such thing as a dewy summer morning in the central San Joaquin Valley of California. By 9 A.M. you're sweating like a pig. Second, my hat gave me a forehead rash. My tomato plants produced about a dozen nice tomatoes and no less than twenty-seven hornworms. If you've ever seen a hornworm, then you know that they're very big. When you look at them, you actually make eye contact. They have to be picked off the plants by hand. This gave me the heebie jeebies. I learned that while one zucchini plant looks very lonely at first; two zucchini plants will feed the neighborhood. Neglect to pick that tender little squash one day and the next day that same squash will shade your house.

I also learned that nothing is cheaper or more abundant in our valley in the summertime than vegetables and fruit. People leave tomatoes on each other's doorsteps in the night. Zucchini are dumped by the side of the road like old tires. So that fall I spaded everything under and turned my energies to herb gardening. Herbs had become quite a fad, and I can usually pick up on fads through osmosis standing next to magazines at the supermarket checkout stands. I became enchanted by the idea of growing my own herbs.

With herbs I could make herbal teas to soothe my senses, soaps to scent my bath, and potpourris to send fragrance wafting through the air. I bought some Birkenstocks and dangly earrings and got to work. I bought all kinds of books on herbs and learned that there are herbs for every purpose. There are kitchen herbs and medicinal herbs, herbs to repel bugs and herbs to attract men. There are more herbs than I had yard to plant them. I had to make some choices. I decided that while growing medicinal herbs might be fine for Dr. Quinn, Medicine Woman, I was Lillian Quaschnick, Drugstore Woman.

Making soap was just ridiculous. And while herbal baths sound very romantic, I don't like leaves and twigs floating around in my bathwater, so that was out, too. But I had big culinary ideas, and lots of frozen zucchini, so I began with a planting of three kinds of oregano, two kinds of marjoram, two tarragon plants, three kinds of thyme, salad burnet, dill, and cilantro.

I planted both borage and foxglove before I realized that while they look a lot alike, one is edible and the other has digitalis in it, which is a heart medication. I chopped both of them down and tossed them, along with my excess oregano and tarragon, on the compost pile, which had by now become a gigantic potpourri. I topped them off with armfuls of lemon balm, lemon verbena, and lemon thyme.

I dried enough basil, oregano, and tarragon to open three Italian restaurants. I made wonderful potpourris with various other herbs and put them in bowls all over the house.

I flavored vinegars and oils for cooking and shared them with neighbors and friends.

I gave bags and jars of everything to everyone. Still, I had herbs to spare.

That winter I went inside, shut the door, and let everything that couldn't fend for itself freeze. When spring came, I took a new tack. I went out and purchased lots of flowers. Nothing edible, nothing medicinal, nothing that did anything but bloom. My yard was full. I learned something new. A little balance. Some produce. Some herbs. A lounge chair, a good book. And lots of flowers to smell.

LILLIAN QUASCHNICK

COMING FULL CIRCLE
WITH MICKEY

When my mother died in a car accident, it took me about twenty-four hours to go over to her condo. This is the home that we had shared from time to time, the place where we gossiped about family matters over salads, shared Christmases, had been best friends.

Next to her bed, still rumpled from her last sleep, was a tiny red Mickey Mouse clock, which I had never seen before. The smiling face of this cartoon was incongruous with the grief that I was feeling, and I wondered when and where she had acquired it. I picked it up, remembering her gentle sense of humor, and decided to take it home with me.

It ran on a single AA battery. Since I didn't know when she bought it, I assumed that the battery would need changing sometime soon. It became part of my life, going with me on overnight trips and ticking away, reminding me of my great pain at the loss of the parent who meant the world to me.

A year later, the little clock was still marking time. It ticked away the hours I spent as the personal rep of her estate, and days devoted to cleaning out her closets, tears falling while I missed my mother. In order to pay the bills on the condo, I gave up my new apartment and moved in, with the clock. It gave me security and made the lonely living there bearable.

Fourteen months after her death, the estate finally settled. I then made changes in my life, signing on as a volunteer at the Atlanta Olympics, breeding my horse, and making plans for a trip to Scotland, the land of my ancestors. Since I had money in the bank, I left my job, seeking time for reflection. I knew that my mother's death had changed me forever, but I wasn't sure who the new me was.

And my mother's Mickey Mouse clock kept ticking.

This was either one heck of a battery, or there was something else to it. I studied the clock, and it came to me that, because life is energy and energy is something that can never die, maybe my mother was trying to tell me something through her clock. I decided, silly as it sounded, that I would keep a close watch on the clock and my life. At the moment that it finally stopped ticking, I would look closely at my environment and my own self, and see if there was something significant to learn at that moment. There would be a lesson.

I made three trips to Scotland, having fallen in love with the country and the sense of purity and security that it gave me. The clock accompanied me each time. During the last trip—a spiritual stay of six months—I rented a mountainside house, hiked, and wrote a book. I dealt with "bats in my cave" and found peace at last. My mother's clock sat on my bedside table at Howeford Cottage and still ticked away on the same battery. I found happiness every morning when I awoke to find it still ticking.

When I came back to the United States, I was at loose ends. I really didn't want to be here; I had found a true home in Scotland. But I made a new home in northern Michigan, in an old log cabin on the edge of the Borealis Forest, and set the clock on a table next to my Buddhist altar. The practice of Buddhism was one I began at the age of nineteen, and it helped me answer a lot of questions about my mother's untimely death. The table was an appropriate place to put her clock.

Five years after my mother died, my father decided to come visit me. This was a total surprise. Visits from him were rare. Although he always tried to understand and be supportive, it was with my mother that I developed my greatest bond. But my father, for his own reasons, had decided to make a quick trip.

It had been about two years since we'd crossed paths. I looked forward to our day together with hope, but not much confidence. We'd always butted heads and never truly understood each other's motivations. I was hoping that we wouldn't argue. I was hoping we'd find some peace and understanding. I was hoping that we could forget the past and develop a new future.

So he and his wife came by in the morning, and we took a drive out to my favorite forest haunts, concluding at the side of Tippy Dam where the salmon run every fall. We talked there of things never once shared between us—the preservation, respect, and conservation of precious natural resources, and the pursuit of dreams. I told him about the struggle I'd had since my mother died, and how I had found some peace in these forests and those of Scotland. It felt to me that Mom was there on the fringes, listening and approving.

He listened to me, and when he spoke, he looked across the waters of the Manistee River, flowing from the dam. As the reflective lights of the river danced across his face, I saw his strength and felt his acceptance of the things that I had done—even though he would have gone about life in other ways. I saw that he was human, no different than the rest of us when it came to emotions and beliefs, but it was hard for him to express them. I felt for the first time that he truly loved me, and realized that although I had lost my mother, I still had one parent left—and a chance to meet him as a daughter, and a friend.

For the first time, we found common ground.

And so it was a mixture of pain and pleasure that I felt as I hugged him good-bye later that afternoon, feeling his aging frailty in my arms for the first time. I realized that time was growing short, but it wasn't lost. I loved my mother, but it was perhaps my father who had taught me the deepest lessons about love, and the pursuit of love.

He drove away. I went back into my house and wandered around for a while, feeling a bit stunned but also feeling a glow never felt before. It was remarkable to learn that I could change this one relationship where change had always seemed impossible. I had one parent left who loved and supported me, and the spirit of that filled my heart. I decided to chant and thank my lucky stars that I had never given up on this relationship.

I knelt at my altar, and glanced at the clock my mother had left me.

It had stopped ticking.

I stared at the dial in disbelief: It said four-ten. That was the exact moment when my father and I had given each other that final hug.

How very significant! It felt like my mother was giving her approval, happy that my father and I had finally found each other. She could go in peace now.

And yes, I chanted, filled with thankfulness, now sure that life is something without beginning or end, and because someone dies doesn't mean they stop caring. I eventually replaced the battery, but not for a few days. I wanted to stare at that clock and remember this lesson.

It's marvelous to me, the way life works itself out. It ticks on, steady and sure, and if we look for mystery and explanation, we can find it, even in the face of a Mickey Mouse clock.

JENNIFER GORDON GRAY

A BOTTLE OF BUBBLES

*E*ach guest at my nephew's wedding was given a two-ounce blue plastic bottle of bubbles and a purple wand, a whimsical substitute for rice or birdseed. The name on the label, "Miracle Bubbles," seemed promising enough. The label also carried the reassuring words "nontoxic," along with a picture of a boy and girl blowing rainbow-filled bubbles: a reminder of the children we once were and a simple pleasure of childhood revisited for an afternoon.

The other guests dipped their wands into the bottles and waved the wands in the air with gleeful abandon, releasing bubble after bubble until they were all gone. But by the time my nephew and his bride made the trek from church to car, most of my bubbles still waited to be released.

Long after the wedding day, I pondered the inevitable question: What should I do with those extra bubbles? I kept waiting for the right moment to wave my own wand in the air and bring new bubbles to life, a moment worthy enough for celebration. Like a watched pot that never boils, the right moment never came. When I moved to the country in the spring, I brought my bottle along, placing it on the dresser in the bedroom.

Although part of me wanted to use up the bubbles, to applaud every day's singular joys, I hesitated. Inertia became my patron saint when it came to the bubbles in my possession.

Perhaps, I told myself, these "genies" stay in the bottle because I do realize that, once they're gone, I can't have them back. Like runaway horses that escape from the barn, these bubbles will never come home again.

A tragedy? Not really. I'd seen plenty of other bottles of bubbles on store shelves. I *could* easily buy any one of them, but something in me knew I wouldn't make the purchase. Other more important items would top my "to buy" list, necessity, once again, prevailing over a pleasure far too frivolous.

And, even if I *did* buy more bubbles, it wouldn't be the same. They wouldn't commemorate a particular occasion, an occasion important enough to give the stamp of approval for a grown woman to play with miracles of the bubble variety.

Sometimes, the entire situation seemed ridiculous. So much time had passed. The bride and groom, now an old married couple with a son, and that souvenir from their wedding still sat on my dresser.

Why all the fuss? It was *only* a bottle of bubbles.

What in the world was I afraid of?

Each morning, I would lie in bed, stare at the blue plastic container and ask myself those questions. The answer finally came, after a rainy night filled with far too many minutes and hours, a night that seemed to offer little consolation.

I'd gone to bed early with a headache. Blasts of thunder had kept me from sleeping. As the gray light of early morning filtered through the bedroom curtains, I heard the steady drumbeats of rain against the window. More thunder rumbled in the distance, threatening a repeat performance. Pain pierced my temples. Aspirin time. I slowly sat up, reached for my robe, and glanced over at the small bottle of bubbles—still half full.

I felt a new sense of comfort as I suddenly realized those bubbles had their own gift to offer, the hope that more moments waited in the future to be applauded, more occasions that would merit a display of miracles.

This memento of past happiness had also become my private crystal ball, a promise of future joys.

Now, each morning, as I prepare to meet the day, I take a glance or two at my bubbles, safely tucked away inside their home. We have developed a relationship of sorts, those bubbles and I.

I have found a use for them after all.

MARY SASS

No one can make you feel inferior without your consent.
ELEANOR ROOSEVELT

THE GIFT OF VALIDATION

Edward Lawrence said I was gorgeous—*validation*
that came fifteen years after my bout with I-gotta-have-
him-itis and a near fatal adolescent crush. Truth is, in ju-
nior high, he didn't even know I was alive. In his mind, I might as
well not have been. I wasn't popular like the other girls, or particularly pretty. I was tall, skinny, kind of funny-looking, and under-
developed. Mother Nature hadn't done her magic yet! To top it
off, I was painfully shy and a bookworm. I was smart as a whip,
but that didn't count for much with boys.

Edward, he was to die for and clearly out of my league in those
days. But I wanted him to like me more than I wanted to be on the
honor roll, more than making the pom-pom squad, more than a
visit from the puberty princess. Every girl wanted Edward. Who
could blame us? He was an oxymoron—a smart jock. Not to mention his great green eyes and sun-melting smile. With his boyish
charm, he could pick and choose, and unfortunately, very few of
us were privileged.

As classmates, he was always cordial and gentlemanly in a
generic sort of way. But he assigned me no more importance than
anyone else and often seemed to look right through me. So years
afterward, with no expressed interest on his part, I finally came to

my senses. I abandoned all fantasies of being his girl. We graduated, went our separate ways, and I found that my crush on him
was replaced by many others.

Over a decade later, as fate would have it, our paths crossed
again. I ran into him during one of my weekly visits to my mom's.
In hip-hugging Jordache jeans and a playfully feminine pastel top,
I felt particularly pretty that day. Strolling along enjoying the summer sun, I noticed someone following behind me in a dark blue
truck. As I picked up my pace, I noticed that my follower picked
up his. I didn't recognize who it was from the distance. To get
my attention the driver blew his horn, and I reluctantly turned
around. Packed in a car full of rambunctious men, there he was.
The sound of my heart was beating louder than my high heels on
the concrete pavement. Through my nervousness, I somehow
managed to wave and smile in acknowledgment.

As he drove farther up the street, he unrolled the car window
and shouted, *"Jennifer Brown, girl you are gorgeous!"* Not wanting to
do or say anything to spoil the moment, I grinned and kept going.

I'll never forget that day. I'll never forget what it did for my self-
esteem. How it made me feel like Cinderella. Since Edward, I have
been affirmed in many, more authentic ways. I have survived the
devastation of divorce, successfully raised a grown son as a single
parent, eluded bankruptcy, attained a college education, purchased a home, and uncovered the secrets to making a mean meat
loaf.

In my younger years, I looked to someone like Edward to af-
firm my bodaciousness. Years later, I see self-love—and the staying power that comes along with it—is what I count on most.

JENNIFER BROWN BANKS

TRUE REWARDS

I searched for my name among the winners even though I knew I wouldn't find my name there. These books had won national acclaim and the big award in children's literature. That gold sticker on a book jacket guaranteed other, better contracts and excellent sales for years to come.

My name wasn't there. My children's books had earned no award.

Oh well, I told myself. *It's just another dumb award. I write for a small company—you know the big publishers have the money to campaign. You know that it's all politics anyway.*

Only this time, I knew those names on the list. They belonged to people I had met at various conferences during the past two years. Each one of them was a nice person, a writer who worked hard at his or her craft—someone like me.

I folded up the newspaper and put the article away. I shrugged and told myself, *You should just be happy they won.*

As a children's book author, I make about two visits a month to local elementary schools and talk about my work as a writer. The usual routine is to talk about myself and then read one of my published books. One of the things I know I do well is reading my books out loud and interpreting all the characters to keep the pace fun for the children. (In another life, I probably would have been a stage actress.)

Usually, I enjoy sharing my books with the young students. But the day the award winners were published in the newspaper, I drove toward a scheduled school visit feeling like nothing would be good enough because I felt down deep inside that I wasn't good enough. Today's performance wouldn't win any awards either.

At the school, I went through the motions of speaking and reading—I was a good actress after all—and after the story time, the librarian asked if any of the students had questions.

There were the usual queries. "Doesn't your hand hurt when you write so much?" "Do you have any pets?" "What's your favorite food?"

I answered with pat, unimaginative answers because the questions were nothing I hadn't heard before. I glanced at the clock in the back of the school cafeteria and felt relieved the time was almost over.

Finally, I saw a thin, black-haired girl in the second row raise her hand ever so tentatively. I saw her tremble and start to lower it again, but I caught her eyes and smiled.

"Do you have a question for me?"

She looked around as if she wanted her teacher's permission to speak, but then she said on her own, "Do you have some stories that nobody wants?"

I realized that she was referring to a comment I had made during my introduction when I talked about revising one novel for five years before I finally placed it with a publisher.

"Yes," I said. "I have some stories that no one wanted. They're in my file cabinet at home."

She didn't hesitate to ask her second question. "Doesn't that make you sad?"

And in my pause, a truth stared me right in the face. Today I was sad; incredibly sad and disappointed. Only when I looked at her little face, I could do nothing but smile. "Yes," I said. "It does make me sad."

Suddenly, I had to tell these children and their teachers the truth about my feelings. I owed it to the kids who had read my story and smiled and clapped and cheered when it was over. I owed them the truth about my mood, because they had to know that sometimes after very hard work, your only reward might be a sad feeling.

"Let me tell you about what happened to me this morning," I told that little girl and all of her friends. "Today I looked in the newspaper and read an article about famous awards that are given to children's books every year. The American librarians select the best books to get this award."

I saw the librarian and some of the teachers nodding.

"Only, my book wasn't on the list. My book didn't win any award. That made me sad too. But I won't stop writing books," I told them. "Even if my stories don't get an award, I'll keep writing them, because I love to write—and because all of you love to read."

I smiled at the little girl, something real and genuine because it was what she deserved. "I think you're my little angel, reminding me why I do what I do. Thank you." And I looked at all of them and said, "Thanks for inviting me to your school. I'm so happy that I came here today."

As their applause ended the program, I felt foolish, and at the same time, I felt as if I had just won first place. I knew the true reward lived in those sixty little faces, in the encouraging smiles of their teachers, and in the compassionate face of the school librarian who probably had selected someone else's book over mine for this year's award.

That day I knew my true reward for writing would probably never be a quote in a slick New York periodical or be celebrated with a gold sticker on my book jacket. I write because I have stories to share. I write because I want to plant a seed for literacy. But most of all, I write because a hopeful child lives inside of me.

DIANE GONZALES BERTRAND

UNDER THE STARS

Camping was never on my list of preferred leisure activities. I always prided myself on being a city person with the secure feel of concrete under my feet. My husband, Tom, who has his roots in the country, still yearns to spend time in the woods. It did not surprise this city girl when he suggested that it would be "fun" for us to spend a weekend camping at a mountain lake. *Lucky me,* I thought sarcastically, *I get to go camping.*

When our camping date arrived, I tackled the important question of what to wear. I own one pair of designer jeans, which had cost a paycheck. Those jeans were not going anywhere near dirt and dung. I packed my Gucci bag with some carefully shopped-for T-shirts, undies, and cosmetics.

My packing complete and with bag in hand, I went outside to the waiting pickup truck. What I saw amazed me. A blue tarp, tied down at each corner of the pickup bed, covered a large mound. I didn't know if we were moving or just going on a weekend camping trip.

"So," I asked Tom, "what's under the tarp?"

"Well, let's see," Tom said, counting off on his fingers. "Sleeping bags, air mattress, camp stove, lanterns, firewood, pots and pans, extra blankets, pillows, towels, ice chest, food . . ."

I've lived in apartments with less stuff than that, I thought, *and I don't like the idea of my kitchen pots and pans going along on this trip.*

We arrived at the lake to find that all the campsites were taken. We were directed to the overflow campground several miles down the hill. I later found out that "overflow" really referred to the chemical toilets.

Tom set up camp in the waning light near a grove of trees, and from the looks of things we were the only campers in the park. I felt a chill as light faded and silence replaced the familiar city sounds of car horns, sirens, and barking watchdogs. This chill was quickly joined by another even more intense shiver, as I was informed that we would be sleeping in the open bed of the truck. No tent, no roof, no cover—no way!

So, Tom suggested that I try sleeping in the front seat of the truck. I climbed in, but I couldn't stretch my legs without bumping into cup holders, a CD player, and storage units. When I curled my legs under me, they immediately went numb, followed by ten minutes of tingling and itching.

"You win," I said, limping to the back of the truck, "but can't we put the blue tarp over us?"

Tom looked at me as if I had just asked for a penthouse suite. "Then you won't be able to see the stars," he said with amazement.

We snuggled into our sleeping bags, which lay on top of an air mattress. Tom began commenting on the clear night, the dark blue sky, and the stars. In the meantime, I focused on the dangers of the dark forest: the escaped felons lurking in the trees, rabid critters carrying the plague, and hillbillies with shotguns.

"Tom," I said, interrupting his starstruck reverie, "did you bring a weapon?"

"No, I didn't bring a weapon," he answered. "You've lived in the city too long. Relax and enjoy the quiet. Go to sleep."

"Tom, there is no way I will be able to close my eyes until I feel safe. We've got to have something we can defend ourselves with if we're attacked."

Tom sighed and worked his way outside the sleeping bag. "The only weapon I can think of, next to force-feeding them the burnt chili beans, is the ax I brought for chopping wood."

He wedged the ax next to the sleeping bag, and we lay on our backs looking at the stars. It had been a long time since I had really looked at a star. What with smoke, smog, fog, and clouds overhead, the city sky had never looked like this. I connected the dots to the Big and Little Dipper and praised them for their synchronism.

A few moments later, I heard a hiss. "What is that noise?" I whispered to Tom. The hiss grew louder. Simultaneously, we began to sink lower in the bed of the truck. I heard Tom groan as he sat up and turned on the flashlight. "It's the air mattress," he said. "I accidentally cut it with the damn ax you made me put in the truck."

My instincts told me this was no time for a smart retort. Headlines flashed, however, through my mind: "DISMEMBERED WOMAN FOUND STUFFED IN AIR MATTRESS; HUSBAND SAYS THE STARS MADE HIM DO IT."

We lay silent for a long time, lost in our own stars, forgetting about the flattening mattress beneath us. We marveled at a shooting star and shared a kiss. I drifted off to sleep under the cover of a starry-night sky, with twinkling lights keeping me safe.

I awoke briefly a few hours later, warm and unharmed, the forest less menacing, the sky a slightly different shade of dark blue. I snuggled closer to my peaceful husband and whispered a fond "thank you" to my guardian stars.

I thought that next time we might bring a telescope and leave the ax by the woodpile. *Next time?* I could sense a smile coming across my face. Here I was—thinking "next time" when, all along, I had been resisting "this time!"

Sometimes magic unfolds under the stars.

CLAUDIA McCORMICK

IX
HOLY
ENCOUNTERS

Out of difficulties grow miracles.

Jean de La Bruyère

DISCOVERING
FREEDOM

Throughout my life, I have often asked myself, "What is freedom?"

I know I am free as long as I obey the laws of the land. Yet, I have continued to wonder why there has remained a twinge of discontent inside my soul. Little did I know the answer would slowly emerge beginning on a Saturday in early April.

Saturday mornings are a welcome sight. I delight in the reality that as long as I am on this planet there will always be another Saturday. I can sit at my desk with a cup of steaming hot coffee where I pray, meditate, and write in one of my several journals. No matter how busy the day, Saturday mornings offer me a short respite from feeling rushed the second the alarm clock goes off the five previous days.

This particular Saturday, my husband went out of town to a coin show. My friend Jackie and I made arrangements to go on a day trip to a quaint town located in the Pocono Mountains.

Prior to that weekend, I had read a short excerpt in one of my magazines that contained a few paragraphs from a book titled *The Practice of the Presence of God*, written in the 1600s by a monk named Brother Lawrence. Although I had no desire to become a nun, or to spend my life in a monastery, I had become captivated by Brother Lawrence's claim that he had discovered the secret of the cultivation of a continual sense of God's presence. I was drawn to his words because I secretly longed to hear a whisper from Him and feel that kind of freedom for myself. I also wanted to find the book. However, my efforts to locate an address for the publisher had been unsuccessful.

Jackie and I left around 8:30 A.M. I welcomed the change of scenery. As we crossed the state line between New York and Pennsylvania, we chattered away, laughing while we caught up with what was going on in our lives.

After a delicious breakfast of bacon, eggs, and pancakes, we decided to browse in antiques shops. We stopped at a few flea markets along the route, before spotting an old house nestled at the bottom of a hilly driveway. Had we not seen the sign KELLY'S AN-TIQUES, we would not have known it was an antiques shop.

We entered the building through two wooden doors with stained-glass windows. Inside the house were shiny wooden floors covered with all kinds of antique furniture. The environment was charming and tranquil. I admired brass beds, hat boxes from years ago resting on mahogany and maple dressers, as well as lace scarves and perfume bottles from the 1800s.

Downstairs, the owner sat on one of the sofas reading a book. We made eye contact, and she smiled. We walked through a small passageway containing an oak desk. To my left was a lit-up glass case with a gorgeous diamond ring inside surrounded by breath-taking antique jewelry.

We then approached a large room in the back with four awesome windows arched at the top. I stood in front of the window on my far left. Outside, I saw a babbling brook with water streaming forth, sparkling in the sunshine. Bare trees surrounding the water were ready to burst forth with leaf shoots at any time. The brook, sunlight, and blue sky framed by the window were breath-taking.

As I listened to music playing softly in the background, I suddenly felt as if I were being uplifted into another world, totally unaware of what was going on around me. For a very brief second, I was in heaven and in touch with God.

The owner gave me permission to take a photo of the babbling brook. As soon as we got into the car, I made a notation in my journal of what I considered to be a magnificent moment in time.

We then went to a bookstore. While Jackie explored another area of the store, I approached a round wire rack full of paperback books. I kept thinking about our visit to the antiques house, and I could not get over the feeling of peace I experienced at that window. Glancing at a small paperback book, my eyes widened when I read the title, *The Practice of the Presence of God* by Brother Lawrence. Astounded, I picked it up. A phrase flashed through my mind: "I give you the desires of your heart, even when you don't ask." I recalled I never did pray for assistance in finding the book. Instantly, I knew that no matter what questions crossed my mind, the Holy Spirit was constantly present in my life.

I purchased the book and shared my experience with Jackie. When I arrived home around dinnertime, I saw a letter lying on the kitchen table written by my pen pal Dalton, from Tennessee. We had been corresponding for five years. I opened his letter and read the following words:

"In my prayer time for you, I saw you and Jesus walking along a pathway by a babbling brook. You were talking animatedly, and He was listening. After you walked a long way, He stopped and gave you a long hug. You both disappeared in a glorious ball of pure light. It was fantastic. I almost cried with joy."

Six years have passed. The book by Brother Lawrence has been read so many times that tape now covers the binding. With the approach of spring, I decided to review my journal entries regarding that special day. I had forgotten that I pasted my photos alongside the story.

I stared at the photo of the trees with the babbling brook in the background of the antique store. Suddenly, on the far right of the picture, I saw it—a small angel, sitting on the branch of one of the trees. Her face was not visible, but she was holding a tiny ball of light in her hands. I immediately remembered the words in my pen pal's letter to me: "You both disappeared in a glorious ball of pure light . . ."

"I wonder if I should share this?" I asked myself out loud, always concerned about what others might think. At that moment, a clear voice said, "You will know when it is time."

I called Jackie, and I told her about the picture and about hearing God's voice. She came over that same day. She, too, spotted the angel in the photo.

The next day the alarm clock startled me at 4:30 A.M. Feeling energetic, I put on my sweat suit, raised the kitchen blinds, and checked the temperature outside. A light snow had fallen overnight.

I began my half-hour walk at 5:05 A.M. All was still except for the crunching sound of my feet in the snow. Fifteen minutes passed and I began backtracking from my original route. As I looked at the imprints I'd left in the snow, it struck me that if they had belonged to someone else, and I tried to walk in them, I still could not be that person. At the same time, I had no right to expect someone else to walk in my footsteps, to think the way I do.

I now know what freedom is. I do not have to hide my Light under a bushel, nor does anyone else. If I have a story to tell, I will do so without concern for what others may think. True freedom is to allow others to be themselves and for me to do the same.

LEA C. TARTANIAN

There's nothing about a woman's
heart that God doesn't understand.
ROMA DOWNEY

MY SPECIAL ANGEL

April 16, 1966, was the happiest day of my life. That is the day that I married my childhood sweetheart. We had been friends since the third grade and had always assumed that one day we would marry and raise a family. Our dreams had come true.

We loved one another from the very depths of our souls and treated each other with respect, kindness, and compassion.

After three years of marriage, I discovered I was pregnant. We were both ecstatic, spending hours in stores picking out clothes, furniture, and accessories for the newest addition to our family.

Our daughter was born on a sunny day in February. It seemed to me that this was an omen. Our family would have a bright future.

For the next ten months we nurtured our daughter, watched her grow, learn to walk, and say her first words. My husband's heart soared the first time she looked at him with her big brown eyes and uttered the word "Daddy." The world had never sounded so perfect.

On our first Christmas with Michelle, we dressed her in a red Santa suit and hat and watched with joy as her eyes lit up at the sight of her first Christmas tree. We lay together later that night and reminisced about the joys of the day and talked of Christmases to come.

In the wee hours of the morning on December 31, my world came crashing down. I awoke to find my husband sitting on the edge of the bed, clutching his chest, and crying out in pain. Before I could throw back the covers and get to him, he began screaming. He stood and staggered into the living room. I followed, fear gripping me, as I asked over and over what was wrong? He never answered. His screams rebounded off the walls of the small room. Suddenly, he fell face first onto the hardwood floor. Then . . . silence.

The deadly sound of the silence seemed even louder than the screams of a moment before. I scrambled for the telephone and called an ambulance. It seemed an eternity before it arrived, but in reality it was a little over four minutes.

After I made the call, I dropped to my knees beside my husband. I shook his shoulder, rolled him onto his back, and called out his name as tears ran down my face and fell onto his. There was no response. As the ambulance pulled into the driveway, siren wailing, I already knew that he was dead.

The next few days were a nightmare. I picked out his casket, made funeral arrangements, and stood by his coffin shaking hands and accepting the sympathetic words of family and friends. I felt no emotion whatsoever at the time. It was if I had turned to stone.

At the cemetery, my father stood beside me, his hand on my shoulder in a gesture of comfort. I knew he was in a lot of pain, too. He and my husband had gotten along splendidly. I couldn't bring myself to comfort him. When they began to lower my beloved husband's casket into the ground, I began to heave deep, gut-wrenching sobs that seemed to tear away my soul. As far as I was concerned, my life was over. Not only had I lost a husband, but also my lover and best friend. It had all happened in the blink of an eye. I leaned against my father's chest while he smoothed my hair with his hand and crooned words of comfort. I remember wondering at the time how the world could be so cruel.

Over the next few weeks, my grieving took on a life of its own. I was angry with my husband for leaving me, angry with God for taking him, and angry at the world in general. For three weeks, I barely slept a wink. Each time I drifted off, I heard my husband's screams. Then I would awaken, trembling uncontrollably, hoping it was all a bad dream. I couldn't eat and wished that I had died with him.

During this period, I stayed at my parents' house, refusing to set foot into my home. I ignored my infant daughter, locking myself in the bedroom of my childhood where I remained for hours, turning a deaf ear to my mother's pleas to come out and join the family.

After a month, my father told me that I either had to go back to my house to live or give the landlord notice that I was moving. I understood his logic, but I wanted nothing more to do with that house. I wrote a notice to terminate my lease and asked Dad to deliver it. I begged him to sell everything in it except our personal belongings. At first my father protested, but finally he gave in. He thought I should face my fears so there would be closure. Again, I refused.

One day just after my daughter's first birthday, Dad made arrangements to meet a used furniture dealer at my house. It seemed as if he was gone for hours, and my imagination ran wild. Had something happened to him? In my sorry state of mind, I felt that the house must be cursed.

When I heard Dad's truck pull into the driveway, I breathed a sigh of relief. All of the reminders of that terrible night would now be gone. I'd never have to go back there again.

My father entered the house looking haggard and drawn. He

took off his coat and hat, hung them up, took a small package out of his pocket, and handed it to me. He told me he had found it in the mailbox at the house.

The return address on the envelope was that of the jewelry shop where my husband and I had purchased our wedding bands. I tore it open, curious as to what was inside. When I dumped the contents, I found an angel pendant about a half-inch high on the finest gold chain I had ever seen. Embedded in one of the angel's wings were three birthstones. An amethyst represented my daughter, a blue sapphire for me, and an emerald for my husband. I looked at Dad. He shrugged. Apparently he knew nothing about it.

It was then I realized that there was still something left in the envelope. The letter inside was addressed to my late husband. It was a letter of apology, indicating that though they had promised Christmas delivery, there had been a delay and they were giving him a partial refund. A check was enclosed along with a handwritten card from my husband. The note read: "This special angel is to keep our family close. When you wear it, always know that I am near."

As I read it, I could feel my husband's presence and almost see the smile on his face. I fastened the chain around my neck, knowing that he would be beside me always to guide me through the trials and tribulations of being a single parent. Peace enveloped me, and in that moment, I knew that for his sake and that of my infant daughter, I must get on with my life.

Luckily for me, Dad had ignored all of my requests. The furniture was still in the small house where my husband and I had lived, loved, and laughed since the day we were married. And the notice to my landlord was still in my father's pocket.

The very next day, I bundled up Michelle and took her back to our house. We were going home.

The grief didn't leave overnight. Sometimes, I would awaken in a cold sweat, frightened and lonely. When this happened, I would hold my special angel between my fingers, rub it gently, then fall into a welcome peaceful sleep.

I lost my special angel some years ago. At first, I was heartbroken. Then, I realized that I no longer needed her in order to feel whole. My only prayer is that the angel found the perfect person who needs her more. She will always be my special angel, and I will never forget that my husband sent her to me from beyond the grave, gently coaxing me back to live and love again.

MARY M. ALWARD

AMAZING GRACIE

T*he week before Christmas, on Monday to be exact,* my husband and our nine-year-old son, Ryan, went out to the driveway to play with a remote control car. It was unusually cold and dark, and I surprised myself by not "mothering" and suggesting they stay in the warm house.

A few minutes later Ryan came running in calling for me. I joined them outside to find a shaken dog obviously seriously hurt by either a vehicle or another animal.

After making several phone calls as quickly as I could, I determined that the Emergency Animal Hospital was the best choice to take the dog. Ryan walked in while I was asking how much the visit would cost. He quickly left the room and returned with a plastic bag full of change and five one-dollar bills.

"Mom," Ryan pleaded, "we have to do something for the dog, and I can pay for it."

"Of course, we'll help the dog, Ryan," I reassured him. "I just need to know what to expect."

The dog was lying still in shock—one leg shattered and the other with cuts. We helped the pup into an animal crate while I gently stroked its back. When we arrived at the animal hospital, a warm and compassionate staff welcomed us.

"What's the dog's name?" the receptionist asked.

"We don't know."

"How was it hurt?"

"We don't know."

"Is it a male or female?"

Still we didn't know.

As we sat down we realized how little we actually knew. After a brief examination, we were informed the dog was a female.

"It was the grace of God that you two went outside on such a dark and cold night," I told my husband and son. "Let's call her Gracie."

Joining other pet lovers in the waiting room, we nervously waited to learn how badly Gracie was hurt. Two hours later, the doctor explained that a car had hit Gracie and with the extent of the injuries, she might not make it through the night. He had given her something for the pain and made her as comfortable as possible. Now, time would tell.

Knowing that we were not the owners, the doctor generously offered the medical treatment and overnight stay at cost. We came to grips with the fact that if we never recovered our $107, we did what was right to do.

Since my name was on the paperwork, I was asked to sign the form approving euthanasia if the doctor determined it was necessary. My heart sank when I completed the form identifying what should be done with Gracie's remains. Leaving the hospital, we said goodbye to the other pet owners we visited with while waiting. They understood what we were feeling. My eyes filled with tears as I turned back to the clinic area and asked Gracie to hold on.

The drive home was quiet. We were tired, drained, and worried at the same time. Ryan suggested that we all pray together. The hope was that Gracie had on a rabies tag. We agreed to return to the animal hospital at 7:30 A.M. in the hope that through the tag the owner would be located.

I could sense that none of us slept well. We tossed and turned. Ryan had a nightmare so we spent some time talking until things settled. We were hoping that Gracie would be there in the morning.

The morning came and my husband went to the animal hospital with strict instructions to call me as I drove Ryan to school. As we headed to school, my cell phone rang.

"Great news!" my husband shared. "Gracie made it through the night. And with her tags, the doctor traced the owners, and they are on their way to the hospital. One more thing, the dog we named Gracie is actually named Shelly."

We were so relieved that Ryan and I cried tears of joy while we drove through the San Antonio traffic.

Before work, I stopped by the hospital just in time to meet Shelly's family. Although stressed, they were relieved to find Shelly alive after hearing the whole story. They told us that they had three dogs, and all three had gotten loose. Izzy came home, Shelly was at the hospital, and Hunter was still unaccounted for. To top it off, they were new to the neighborhood. What a terrible way to spend their first Christmas season in their new home!

At the end of what seemed like a long day, my husband noticed a woman driving slowly on our street. She hesitated, parked, and walked toward our front door.

"Did you find a dead dog in front of your house?" she asked as my husband greeted her.

"Dead no, injured yes," my husband responded as he told her what had happened.

She explained that she had seen the accident and that she'd captured Hunter, but Shelly was injured and ran from her to somewhere around our house. Now Shelly, Izzy, and Hunter would all soon be home!

I marveled at the miraculous way each step had unfolded as though planned with divine precision to gently bring this story to a joyful ending. We have talked with Shelly's parents a few times for updates on her condition. They were kind enough to cover the expenses we paid at the Emergency Animal Hospital. They also sent us a beautiful gift basket to wish us a Merry Christmas and thank us for all we did for Shelly. I can't think of a better way to celebrate the spirit of Christmas.

The best gift will be when Shelly goes home from the hospital, and we can deliver the three dog bones that sit under our Christmas tree with the names of Izzy, Hunter, and . . . Shelly, although she will always remain Gracie in our hearts.

JAYNE GARRETT

LESSONS FROM A
BOX OF TOYS

I t was winter in Wisconsin, the air cold and crisp. I watched my two children make a path through the deep snow and climb aboard the school bus. I said my usual prayer that my children would arrive at their destination safely.

I picked pajamas off the bathroom floor and hung forgotten towels. It seemed to be a day like all the rest and when the phone rang, I was not surprised. A friend and I talked almost daily after our children left for school.

Today, though, was not the normal conversation, but news that left me with the feeling of a dark cloud hovering over me.

During the night, a family in our small community had lost their home to a fire. Two small children, about the ages of my kids, had been in that house. They escaped the blaze, but just barely. Their home was a total loss. This kind of news always saddens me, but even more so such a short time after the holidays. My heart felt heavy. I wanted to reach out and help these people, yet not knowing them personally, I couldn't think of anything appropriate to do.

My kids, Hannah and Beau, arrived home hungry to tell me the story of the fire. We shared our concerns and talked about how the young victims of the fire didn't have their Christmas presents, they didn't have any toys to play with.

Their sad eyes looked at me for answers. They wanted to feel better, and I was supposed to provide that comfort for them. It was a tall order to fill. I suggested they say prayers for the family and explained that no one had been hurt. That was the most important thing. However, it wasn't enough for them so I suggested they each find a nice toy to give to the children. They seemed overjoyed with the idea.

Beau and Hannah were up the stairs like tiny bolts of lightning while I started dinner preparations. The dark cloud that had been over me all day seemed to have cast a deeper shadow after seeing my children so glum.

A half-hour later, Beau appeared at the bottom of the steps asking for a box. I directed him to the closet where I had stuffed some extra ones after Christmas. I was a bit curious as he went up the stairs dragging a large box, and came back down for another. Soon he was down again, rummaging in the closet, and went back up with paper bags.

I could hear enthusiastic voices floating down the staircase, but could not make out the conversation.

Their dad called and would be late for supper, so I put food on their plates and told Hannah and Beau it was time to eat.

Usually slow to get to the table, I was shocked to see them come immediately. They giggled while they ate, and the looks they gave one another made me slightly suspicious. I was relieved to see that their mood had lightened, yet curious as to what was going on.

Before I could ask, they began firing questions at me. Where are the kids whose home had burned staying tonight? Could we call them? Could we visit them?

I assured them I had no idea where they might be and that a visit might not be appropriate. They pressed me for answers, and I finally found out why.

They bounded up the stairs. I peeked around the corner and saw both children, each struggling to carry a big box and a bag down the steps. Reaching the bottom, they announced, "We are giving these toys to the kids whose house burned down."

I looked in amazement at the amount of stuff they had collected. Cars, trucks, dolls, stuffed animals, and books. I noticed some of the things they had chosen were gifts they had received at Christmas. They insisted those kids needed these toys now, tonight.

I looked into their happy, loving eyes and knew this was one of the most important things they would ever do. I knew that these gifts were truly from a deep place within their young hearts. They were not only giving toys but also giving of themselves. I saw them paving a way of life for themselves.

A few phone calls later I had found out where Beau's and Hannah's gifts could be delivered.

We snuggled into our warm jackets and pulled on our boots. There was snow falling lightly on our cheeks as we made our way to the car. As we drove into the night, I thanked God for giving me two extra-special gifts and for giving me the opportunity to be in the company of such loving, caring, beautiful little people. As we drove into the night, I didn't feel the cold of winter, but the warmth of true and honest love.

LINDA ASPENSON-BERGSTROM

Reality is something you rise above.
LIZA MINNELLI

HIGH-ALTITUDE BELIEVING

I love to fly! A wave of pure freedom washes over me every time the wheels of the airplane gently lift away from the earth. My feeling of elation grows as I rise from the ground. I knew I'd become a pilot after I took an introductory flight. I worked two jobs while I took flight lessons, one to support me, the other to support my flying.

Although I had to study aerodynamics, aircraft loading, fuel requirements, navigation, weather, aircraft systems, airspace designations, aviation regulations, and much more to become a pilot, it was worth it.

Like any other group of people who share mutual interests, pilots tend to find each other. A few years ago, I had the great good fortune to live in a community where there were several other women pilots, including my friend Mary. Mary and her husband had their own Piper Cherokee, and I was flying an airplane that belonged to my father until he passed away.

Mary's husband flew to a neighboring state one day in late July, and before he could return, thunderstorms had rolled into the area. He didn't have time to wait for the weather to clear because he was needed back at work, so he rented a car and drove home. A couple of weeks later, I gladly volunteered to fly Mary in my dad's

Sundowner to bring their stranded Cherokee back home. We decided that on the return flight we'd fly our airplanes in loose formation.

We departed the home airport a little after 8 A.M. the following
Saturday. The weather was perfect for the flight—smooth air,
good visibility. A high, thin cloud layer diffused the sunlight. As we
climbed away from the airport, we could see horizon to horizon.

After about twenty-five minutes, I turned the controls over to
Mary and opened a chart to verify my next visual checkpoint. At
that same moment, the airplane began shaking violently from
side to side. It was apparent that something had gone wrong with
the engine. The tachometer indicated that it had lost a few hundred RPMs. I took the controls from Mary, trying to determine
what was wrong. Light airplanes have the ability to glide for significant distances, but one thing was for sure: we didn't have
enough power to maintain altitude.

After checking all of the engine controls for any malfunction
that we might have inadvertently caused, I dialed up the fre-
quency for Seattle Center and declared an emergency. I wanted
someone to know where to find us.

Mary and I had both been looking for a place to land. Unfortunately, there weren't any great prospects. We were in the middle
of nowhere. The nearest airport was twenty-four miles away, beyond our gliding range. The terrain was mountainous and covered with trees. There were no roads. I spotted a railroad track
that was being dismantled, but the piles of railroad ties made that
unusable. The only other long, straight, man-made structure was
a canal, also unsuitable for landing.

I had handed Mary the emergency landing checklist and asked
her to make sure that I had not missed anything. We glided over a
ridge and spotted a large, somewhat flat clearing. It looked like
open range; there were a few dozen cattle scattered here and
there. We had been gradually descending, and it became our best

hope for an impromptu runway. A grim thought crossed my mind; at least it would be easy for Search and Rescue to locate the wreckage in such a wide-open area.

Even though we were busy flying the airplane and setting up for a landing, a myriad of thoughts crossed my mind. I was single, but Mary had a husband and two young sons. I had to make sure that she made it home to them. And then, a silly thought: *Uh-oh, I wish I had rewritten my will!* The words of my flight instructor jolted me back, "Keep flying the plane."

I determined from which direction I wanted to land and maneuvered the plane so that we would touch down with plenty of clear ground in front of us. I felt grateful that this one place had no trees or bushes or livestock. We carefully monitored our airspeed. We wanted to slow for the landing, but didn't want to stall and crash.

As I made the turn to my final approach, Mary and I were low enough to see details in the terrain that we could not detect before. I gulped. It was very rocky. The grass and weeds were taller than I'd thought and had hidden the rocks until we got closer. My hopes for a soft touchdown and rollout evaporated. I expected the airplane would cartwheel and tumble at least once before coming to rest, most likely on fire. I quietly swore and said, "God help us." Then we both fell silent as our precious altitude ran out, and the inevitable moment of contact arrived.

I stayed on the controls, pulling the nose up at the last second just as I would have on a runway. Mary was holding on, too, in case the controls were wrenched from my hands. Our right main tire hit first, and the airplane pivoted to the right. The left wing came up about five degrees, and we were now bouncing and scraping from our right to our left. The propeller struck the ground and quit turning. On the final bounce, the left wing came down and we came to rest.

I yelled, "Bail out!" but it wasn't necessary. Mary didn't even remove her headset; she lunged out the door and the set popped off when it reached the end of its cord. We both hit the ground running in case the airplane burst into flames.

The airplane was totaled. Although it remained upright, the violence of the crash landing caused extensive damage. With the landing gear gone, the engine had been stopped in the most destructive way, and the airframe was tweaked beyond repair.

Between us, we had one injury. I broke a nail.

I will never, ever forget that day. It was the day that I learned that I have the ability, the confidence, and the courage to make good decisions, to keep my wits about me in the face of almost certain death, and to remember everything I'd learned to get me through such an ordeal. I never, in my most awful dreams, had entertained the idea that I might be faced with such a huge challenge.

My life is different now. I savor things that I used to take for granted. I look at my friends and family with gratitude that I still have time to spend with them. And even though we live many states apart now, I have a unique friendship with Mary that both of us hope to never eclipse with another life-threatening event.

Four days later, I got into another little airplane and started flying again. I had to—flying is what I love to do. Besides that, I believe in myself and that alone is very freeing. It makes all the difference in the world.

DENA McCLUNG

THE EMISSARY

My family gathered in the sweltering living room, the grief palpable and smothering like a heavy wool blanket. We met in my parents' home—my step-brothers, their wives, and I—the day following the funeral of my brother, my only sibling. He had tragically taken his own life in a moment of despair that I can never hope to understand.

As I sat in deep introspection, holding on to my infant daughter as if my life depended on her, an insistent *mrr-oww* startled me. I looked around the room at the others who had similarly been lost in their thoughts, and their faces seemed to reflect my confusion about what we were hearing. No cats lived in my parents' house.

I opened the front door, and there on the threshold sat a small tortoise-shell cat, her black coat speckled with orange and white, as if fire and snow had burst in a midnight sky. *Mrr-oww,* she repeated, looking at me expectantly.

"What is it?" my stepmother Paulina asked.

"It's a cat . . . and she's acting as if she wants to come in," I answered hesitantly.

"Well, *let* her in," she replied. I did a double take at Paulina since this was totally out of character for her; she's allergic to cats! But I did as bidden.

The little cat entered the house as if she knew exactly what she was doing and had been there before. Even the dogs didn't concern her. This was where she was meant to be, she seemed to be saying, as she entered the room and entered our lives. Making a circuit around the room she greeted us each in turn, jumping onto our laps, then looking directly into our eyes as if reading our minds. Caressing our arms and legs with her silken coat, she emanated compassion and tenderness, as if knowing exactly what we needed. How could this small cat be so comfortable with strangers? I asked myself.

When the stifling heat of the house became unbearable, my sisters-in-law and I headed outside to feel the refreshing light breeze in the shade kiss away our sweat and sorrow. The little tortie—definitely not feeling like a stranger to us anymore—followed and curled up on the grass where we sat, the babies asleep on a blanket next to us. Every now and then she would rise and come again to touch us gently with her paw, as if saying, "You will be all right. You are strong and can make it through this. I am here."

For hours we talked about my brother, our memories, the unanswered questions . . . the what-ifs and if-onlys. And we talked about the cat. Where had she come from? I had never seen her before. Why did she choose *this* house to visit? Was she an angel sent from God to give us comfort? Or could she be the spirit of my brother, returning to make sure we were okay?

And then one of my stepbrothers came out to join us and saw the cat next to the peacefully sleeping children. Not aware of our discussion and unsure of what the tortie might do to the babies, he chased her away. *No,* my heart cried, *don't go, don't go.* But it was too late. She had disappeared from my sight. Heartbroken, I felt as if I couldn't breathe. She was gone. *He was gone.*

The afternoon turned into evening, and I prepared to go home to my husband and son. I looked once more for the tiny tortoiseshell cat, but she remained hidden. After I left, she did return to my parents' house, spending several hours lying on the chair behind Paulina's shoulders and sitting on my father's lap. And when darkness came, she went outside and disappeared into the night.

I'll never know for sure what possessed that beautiful little cat to appear at the door when we needed so desperately the comfort she gave. I believe that God sends messages to us in a variety of ways. Maybe she *was* an angel. Or perhaps, somehow, she did embody my brother's spirit. What I do know is that the small cat who wasn't afraid to go over a threshold, who tenderly caressed each one of us in turn, had brought me a great deal of peace and solace and strength. And the feeling that I'd experienced a miracle. That maybe, just maybe, for a brief moment in time, I'd felt the gentle touch of my brother once again.

LISA ROBERTSON

SNOW ANGEL

Minnesota winters are harsh. You need to work together because when the wind comes out of the northwest and the skies open up and dump several inches of snow in your yard, you had better be ready. Everyone has a digging-out plan for those infamous winter storms. After twenty-one years of marriage I found myself without a plan facing winter.

Officially, my husband and I had separated shortly before Christmas. Unofficially it had been over for several years. But even in those years leading up to the separation I could always count on him to plow our 150-foot driveway. Now it was part of the preliminary settlement; I got the house and along with that the responsibility of plowing the drive. I was scared to ask for help, and so I didn't.

On the outside I said, "I don't need anyone. I can do this." Inside I heard myself saying, *Who would you ask anyhow? No one really cares about all of this. You really are alone!*

God heard my soul crying and blessed us with a kind Minnesota winter until late January when my luck ran out. Snow fell in the many inches category. But I was stronger now. I could do this. I was my own plan. I grabbed my shovel and told myself the exercise would be good. That the fresh air I would be inhaling was going to benefit my stay-by-the-fire winter personality. So, shovel in hand, muffler around my neck, and enough layers of clothing to make the Michelin Tire man look thin, I headed out into the subzero freeze, ready for the drifts and all that exercise.

I started with the snowplow furrow at the end of my driveway. Twenty minutes into that, I had not even made a dent. I wanted to give up, and I kept shoveling. I wanted to buy a snowblower, and I kept shoveling. I wanted someone to come along and offer to help, and I kept shoveling. I didn't want to be my own plan, and I prayed.

And out of the east came a pickup truck. You know the kind: big get-out-of-my-way plow on the front end, hydraulics to lift that monster shovel, and headlights bright enough to light up midnight on a moonless night. I kept shoveling until that "cowboy snow angel" turned in with his pickup doing what it was made to do. I recognized my friend from long ago, and I stepped to the side.

We had gone to high school together, sat behind each other in advanced topics, walked across the stage on graduation day as classmates twenty-five years ago, and congratulated each other when we started our married lives.

I watched as back and forth he went, kicking up snow and clearing the drive. Frozen tears collected on my eyelashes as I stood leaning on my baby shovel. For the very first time since December, I understood it wasn't the whole world that I had separated from. It was just my husband. I was overwhelmed with the idea that people like my snow angel were still a big part of my life and would always be there ready to help.

As he backed out for the last time, he tipped his hat to me, lit a cigarette, and continued west into the night. I watched his taillights disappear down the frozen highway, and I thanked God for sending me my snow angel and letting me know that I was not alone.

He wasn't home when I called to thank him. I spoke with his wife and cried as I told her how much I had appreciated his kindness. I laughed a nervous laugh when I said that he might have to be part of my winter plan. She understood and reassured me that both of them were my friends and would help whenever they could. I talked with snow angel shortly after that. His slow easy smile spread across his face when I thanked him and told him how much I had hated to ask for help. "I go by your house every day to work. I'll be glad to swing in and clear your driveway for you."

And so for the last three years he has continued to be my snow angel. Not one winter storm has snowed me in thanks to him. Even though I have tried to pay him, in the tradition of great cowboys, he continues to tip his hat and ride into the sunset. And as I watch his disappearing pickup melt into the horizon, I am at peace knowing God has blessed me with true friends to help me through this life.

ELIZABETH KRENIK

X
ON THE
LIGHTER SIDE

Women complain about premenstrual syndrome,
but I think of it as the only time of the month that I can be myself.

ROSEANNE

THE MANNEQUIN

Years ago, I couldn't wait to travel across country and visit my friend Marie in Southern California. We were both in our early fifties with time on our hands, and she decided now was the time for her to show me the sights.

Marie not only took me to the usual tourist places such as Rodeo Drive, Knott's Berry Farm, Disneyland, and movie studios, but also to a wardrobe factory where you could buy clothes off the rack at wholesale prices. And she knew of resale shops that stocked only clothes that had been worn by the stars.

The day we visited Grauman's Chinese Theater to view the famous footprints was warm and sunny. The theater was set back about twenty feet from the sidewalk. At the entrance stood a young male model holding a mannequin pose. His attire was a cross between a cowboy and an Indian brave. His pants and vest were of light tan leather. The absence of a shirt showed the muscularity of his arms. His skin was the color of bronze. He wore a hat that looked worn and weathered atop his black hair. In front of his feet a pouch of coins laid open to view. His brown eyes were in a fixed stare straight ahead, and he didn't move a muscle as people passed by him in both directions.

I found it intriguing. I stood directly in front of him and said, "It's nice to make your acquaintance, and you are?" Then I turned to Marie and asked, "Do you suppose he would move if we tried to make off with the coins?" I smiled at him and said, "You're just my kind of man—the strong silent type." I was truly enjoying that I had him at a disadvantage.

We moved on and viewed the footprints we had come to see. By the time we left, there were many more people milling around. As we started to pass the mannequin, I stopped and asked, "Did you miss us?" Then added as my parting comment, "Ah, how soon they forget." One split second later, he grabbed me, threw my head back, and planted a long kiss on my very surprised lips. After which, he resumed his pose and stared straight ahead. Some people laughed while others applauded. I stumbled forward in my much-deserved embarrassment.

Let me say I found Rodeo Drive interesting, and I enjoyed the resale shops of the stars. No one appreciates a wholesale price tag more than I do. But if I could have a do-over, I'd take Grauman's Chinese every time.

EDNA MINER LARSON

MOM'S MAKEOVER

After working long hours all week at our veterinary clinic in town, I was looking forward to spending Saturday afternoon just resting. I went upstairs and lay down on the bed with a good mystery paperback, and thought to myself, *I'll just read until I get sleepy.* That lasted about ten minutes.

Erin found me first. She said she was just checking to see if I needed anything (little angel). I assured her that I didn't, but she obviously wanted company—so I told her she could sit on the bed with me.

She suggested that she could braid my hair. Erin has quite a collection of little barrettes and things, and went running to get her bag of goodies. Soon I had a mass of colorful dragonflies, ladybugs, and butterflies pinned across my head.

Then came some serious pampering. She brought out her older sister's collection of fingernail polish bottles. There was quite an assortment, so while I read my book, she cheerfully chattered away about important this-and-that things while painting my nails.

Soon little brother Austin wandered into the room, and not to be outdone, started "beautifying" Mom in his own way. While Erin painted my toes, Austin applied some of his small dinosaur tattoos to my arms, then set about unraveling my braids and attempting his own hair creations. I think most of it amounted to knot tying.

I thought, *Why would anyone pay good money to get pampered at a spa? What they really need is a couple of young children and a Saturday afternoon.* No mom ever had more attention paid to her than I did that day.

The moment came that my little ones had worked so hard for. I was helped off the bed and led to the mirror. All ten fingernails were painted different colors, with a topcoat of sparkle added for brilliance. All ten toes were painted a fiery bright red (I later found out the color was called Panic Button). Spikes of hair stood out from my head pointing nine different directions, and green dinosaurs were liberally applied to my arms. It was unanimously decided that I was breathtaking.

The afternoon was now spent, and I went downstairs to start supper. That's when my husband looked up from his recliner, raised his eyebrows, and told me that I should get leather pants and a Harley motorcycle to go along with my new look.

Okay, so brilliant and flashy is not my style. That evening I took off the fingernail polish, rubbed baby oil on the tattoos until they were gone, then brushed the tangles out of my hair. In a few minutes time, I was back to normal—almost.

Already eagerly looking forward to my next day of rest, yet not quite ready to let go of this one, I decided to leave my toenails red for a few more days.

PAMELA JENKINS

If life is a stage, I'd like better lighting.
AUTHOR UNKNOWN

A SHOPPING SPREE

"**I**'ve got to go to Kroger's," Roxanne complained, rolling up a forkful of linguine Alfredo during one of our weekly dinners. "There's no milk for breakfast even."

These standing dates had revitalized our then-ten-year-old friendship and strengthened it to steel as we simply shared lives, the mundane and the monumental.

"Grocery stores are the best places to meet guys."

"I'm married." She pushed pasta into her mouth.

"I'm not, and it is your duty as a happily married woman to make sure all your friends, especially your best friend"—I waved my fork at myself—"find the same joy and fulfillment you have."

She laughed, but after dinner we were strolling through Kroger's automatic door. We were a distinct pair as she pushed a shopping cart, and I rolled behind in my wheelchair.

Roxanne picked through the produce—some grapes, a couple of bananas—before moving on. I followed chattering, reading labels, and watching people. Then it happened—right in the middle of the breakfast cereal.

He was drop-jaw, feet-stuck-to-the-floor gorgeous and nearly landed in my lap after dodging Roxanne in front of me. Sandy hair, not too long, and eyes I could've sworn were teal. His lips moved, and I guess he apologized, but I didn't hear a word. I was too busy taking in every inch of him.

When I came to, Roxanne was out of sight. I raced to catch up, knocking the back of her legs with my wheelchair's footstools. "Did you see that?" I hissed.

"What?"

"Only the most beautiful male person on the face of this earth! How could you miss him?"

She shrugged. "I was checking my list."

I rolled my eyes and trudged behind her, completely disappointed in the potential of my best friend. As she perused the meat cooler, I trolled in a wide arc like a bored child, peeking down the aisles for a second look.

"There he is!" I hissed again. He stooped in front of snack chips, looking for his brand.

"Oooh! Nice." Roxanne looked up from the meat as he squatted for a package on the bottom shelf. My faith had been restored.

"Think his eyes are really that color?" I asked as we hurried on, not wanting to get caught in our game.

"How could you see his eyes from there?"

"No, before. They're teal!"

She laughed in a loud burst. "It's probably just the shirt!"

Roxanne spotted him next by a display of soft drinks. She offered to go around to the other side and trap him.

"O.K.!"

She turned to me with mock horror, then grinned.

"Well, that would be funny!" I laughed.

He showed up at the dairy cooler next, poking through the stacks of cheese. I motioned at Roxanne to look, but she already was. We shared a conspiratorial glance, then giggled with a "let's not go there."

We lost him when Roxanne ran into some friends. I smiled but kept my eyes peeled for our prey. No sign of him. Our game was at its end.

"I told you, you never know who you'll meet in the grocery store."

"We didn't meet him," Roxanne said as she checked her list. "We stalked him."

"Yeah, well—you've never had this much fun before, have you?"

"Not in Kroger's," she quipped, then returned to the produce department for some forgotten broccoli.

Directly across from the checkout lanes, the produce area offered a clear view to the other end of the store. I parked myself behind a basket of children's balls on clearance. It's hard to hide a 150-pound power wheelchair anywhere, but behind the basket I didn't look too obvious.

"Roxanne!" He pulled around the cigarette display and was heading for the registers.

"Come on! We can get behind him in line!" I almost shouted at her. She was still picking out broccoli. Wait. He parked his basket and disappeared down an aisle. He had forgotten something—a reprieve.

"Look at you!" Roxanne stuffed her precious broccoli into a plastic bag, laughing at me. I stuck my tongue out but kept on the lookout.

"He's getting in line!"

"What's the difference between this broccoli and that one, fifty cents cheaper?" She unstuffed her bag and reached for the other green bunch. The man of my dreams was getting away and she was picking out broccoli!

When we got to the checkout, I figured he was long gone, but undying optimism drew my eyes over the row of registers and customers. He was two lanes over, writing a check. I had to bump Roxanne twice before she looked. She grinned and shook her head.

"Left-handed," I whispered. She shot me a look, but no comment. He was still at the counter when we led the bag boy to the van. "No ring."

Outside, I kept watch to see where my teal-eyed hero would go. There was no sign of him as Roxanne unfolded the lift to get me in the car.

"I must have missed him," I said and took one last look out the back window. "There he is!" He stopped at an SUV loaded with kids.

"Maybe he's baby-sitting," I said with hope, watching him open the front door, handing his bags in. "They must be his nieces and nephews," I rationalized. "We could follow him to see if he lets them out somewhere."

Roxanne whirled, wide-eyed.

"I'm just kidding!"

"Good," she chided, " 'cause I've got milk in here. We can't go chasing after some guy with milk in the car!"

I watched him drive out of our lives, clueless to the game we had shared or how our fate was sealed by a half gallon of milk. Roxanne never took me grocery shopping again.

AMY MUNNELL

TECHNOLOGY FOR THE MILLENNIUM

❧

I read a survey recently that asked people what they thought was the most important creation of the last century? Most people chose the computer. Others answered antibiotics, rayon, or indoor toilets. I have to disagree with them all and say right up at the top of the list ought to be that wondrous invention—duct tape. Yes, I said duct tape.

Think about it. If you can't fix it with duct tape, it can't be fixed. On my commute to work along a fairly busy road going to Durham in North Carolina, I see a large black mailbox that gets knocked off its post on a regular basis. At different times, the homeowner tries reattaching his box. Within a couple of weeks, there it is lying all banged up on the ground. About three months ago, I saw the dented box stuck sideways on its perch, held on by three loops of duct tape. I thought to myself, *Good for you. Now it won't go anywhere.* And it hasn't. A vandal would have to stop and cut that baby off.

Years ago, I lived in a trailer so dilapidated that when pieces of molding or siding came off, it was impossible to nail them back. If you walked down the narrow hallway with a heavy foot, the paneling would pop right off the wall. Slam a door and you would be holding a doorknob. I repaired cabinets, caulked windows, and insulated pipes. For two years, 10 percent of my paycheck went to Super Glue and duct tape. My friends still tease me about the home I had with duct tape interior.

My youngest daughter came home the other evening and said she needed help with a science project due the next day. I told her

I would help after she swore that she had just gotten the assignment and had not, in fact, known about this for weeks. (Another story for some other time.)

She had to make something to place a raw egg in that could be thrown from fifty-two feet (the height of the gym) and not break the egg. After our elaborate plan to build a wooden box fell through, we had to come up with a Plan B.

My Plan B was a small cardboard box filled with scrap fabric and covered with duct tape. The following is the loving exchange between mother and daughter working side by side:

"What is that?"

"It's your project."

"That's the dorkiest thing I have ever seen."

"It's the best I can do. It will work. It's going to be covered with duct tape. Look."

"I am not taking that to school. I just won't take anything."

"You will get a zero. Fail your grade. Live with me forever. Besides, I heard race car drivers tape their fenders back on with this stuff. Beautiful, isn't it?"

"I'll take a zero."

"Duct tape is the ultimate equalizer. I can accomplish the same thing as a veteran carpenter, a truckload of tools, and two helpers with a roll of duct tape and a bent butter knife."

"I wish I lived in a normal home."

"Ta da!"

"I hate my life."

When I picked her up this afternoon, she informed me right off that her egg was intact.

Duct tape. Technology for the millennium.

LEIGH SENTER

SWEEPSTAKES DREAMING

*I*burst out laughing when I opened the mail one morning to find this sweepstakes letter:

> ?Dear Lilian Queaqscnick,
> *IF YOU HAVE AND RETURN THE WINNING NUMBER
> PRIZE SEAL, WE'LL BE HAPPY TO SAY . . .*
> *LILIAN QUEAQSCNICK, YOU'VE MADE THE FINAL
> CUT—YOU'RE ONE OF TEN LUCKY PRIZEWINNERS GUAR-
> ANTEED TO WIN UP TO $13,000,000!*
> *IMAGINE YOURSELF, LILIAN QUEAQSCNICK, DRIVING
> DOWN JAMESON AVENUE IN YOUR BRAND-NEW GOLD
> ROLLS-ROYCE!*
> *THIS CAN BE A REALITY, LILIAN QUEAQSCNICK, IF YOU
> RETURN THE WINNING NUMBERS IN OUR $13,000,000
> GIVEAWAY!*

I'm a middle-aged, middle-class, middle-income former high
school teacher, mother, and grandmother. I need a new kitchen
floor, and I'd like to paint the middle bedroom. My husband needs
a new pickup. He also needs some rest.

How did the sweepstakes people know that my secret dream is
to have a *brand-new Rolls-Royce* to drive around the neighborhood?
And gold nonetheless! Wow, they sure do know what buttons to
push to get my attention!

Maybe I, *Lilian Queaqscnick,* could also have a *brand-new dia-mond tiara* to wear when I drive my *brand-new Rolls-Royce* to the supermarket.

I opened the huge envelope with the check in the window. *Pay to the order of Lilian Queaqscnick amount: $13,000,000.*

Too bad it's a bogus check. Too bad my name is Lillian Quasch-nick.

There is a letter enclosed telling me who the previous winners are. *Myrtle Schmertz of Winnie, Illinois, won $5,000,000.* I don't know what to do with this bit of information. Is this so I can give Myrtle a call and ask her if she did indeed win before I spring for a stamp to mail this entry form? Or maybe they think I know Myr-tle. I fish around the inside of the envelope. There's enough sticky stamps, colored dots, scratch and sniff, and cut and paste para-phernalia to entertain a first grade class.

There's the *Yes; I want a chance to win $13,000,000!* sticker. This has to be glued to the upper left side of the entry blank. There's stick your megabucks red circle here if you want your name included as a finalist. (Duh!) This goes on the outside of the envelope. And the *please enter me in the $100,000 bonus Sweep-stakes* sticker that goes to the right on the entry form if I order magazines and want to be entered in the bonus round. There are the three squares for pasting magazine selections in order of preference. If I don't order magazines, I have to scratch the one of the three silver seals that matches my entry form color to enter me to win one of three lovely prizes whose descriptions are on the backside of the form in small print. But if I don't order magazines, I have to find three 3 × 5 cards to write my name and address and twelve-digit entry number on and send those in an envelope that doesn't have the special superduper seal on it.

I'm beginning to wonder if all this work is worth $13,000,000. I think I'll write them a letter:

Dear SWEEPSTAKES PEOPLE,

Imagine me opening up a sweepstakes letter that enters me in a contest to win $2,000,000. Actually, $1 million would be just fine—$13 million gives me a headache. Use the other $11 or $12 million to make another eleven or twelve people happy and increase my chances of winning. Tell me to imagine myself paying off my bills and living in retirement with my well-rested husband. Give me just one box to check that says:

PLEASE ENTER MY NAME TO WIN ANY AMOUNT OF MONEY YOU WISH TO GIVE AWAY.

Imagine me sending it right back to you, maybe even with a magazine order or two.

Sincerely,
Lillian Quaschnick

LILLIAN QUASCHNICK

*As time passes we all get better at blazing a trail
through the thicket of advice.*
MARGOT BENNETT

THE HUNT FOR
WILD ASPARAGUS

When we were told that there is a place in the Nebraska sandhills where wild asparagus grows in abundance, my husband and I were determined to find it. Having done some fishing in rivers nearby, we felt sure we could handle this type of venture and looked forward to the trip.

Our friends, Roz and Ted, heard about our plans and asked if they could join us. We were concerned because both of them were nearing eighty years of age (nearly ten years our senior), and neither had our experience in meeting the challenges of outdoor life. However, since we considered ourselves quite knowledge-able, it was decided that we could guide them through the various pitfalls.

It was a beautiful morning when we loaded our gear into the station wagon and began the drive toward our destination. We stopped in a small town for breakfast and continued our journey in high spirits.

We finally arrived at the designated area and were overjoyed to see wild asparagus growing in the pastures and along the fence rows. We parked the station wagon by the side of the road and made plans to start our expedition.

In this part of Nebraska, cattle ranching is the main occupation so the pastures are usually well grazed. The branches of giant cottonwood trees form canopies over narrow graveled roads and make a unique, pleasant sound as their heart-shaped leaves move against one another in response to the wind. Traffic is almost nonexistent. Waterfowl, red-winged blackbirds, bluebirds, and many species of wildflowers are all common, and it's not unusual to spot a deer or a red-tailed hawk.

But there is another side to this peaceful appearing environment. Because the ground water level is so high, the deep roadside ditches are always flooded. There are some biting insects, poison ivy grows as abundantly as the asparagus, and there are barbed-wire fences around all the pastures. It is also necessary to remember to step carefully in places where cattle have been grazing.

After we had all used insect repellent and sunscreen, my husband and Ted left together with their buckets while Roz and I chose an opposite route. We found a place where a large tree had fallen over a ditch that separated us from a pasture, which appeared to be full of asparagus. Thinking it the safest way across, I sent Roz first while I held her bucket and gave advice about using extreme caution.

Once she was on the other side, I stepped out on the log carrying a bucket in either hand. Unfortunately, my right foot slipped, and I lost my balance and fell headfirst into the ditch full of water. I came up sputtering and embarrassed, but still clutching the much-needed pails. With some help from my friend, I climbed out and gave thanks that the only thing injured was my pride. We had all brought along a change of clothing, and I knew the sun would soon warm me up quickly.

Next we had to cross a barbed-wire fence, so I held the lower wire down with my boot so Roz could crawl through. She made it easily; but when my turn came, I ripped my trousers and scratched my thigh deeply enough to be grateful that my tetanus shot was up-to-date.

My misfortunes were forgotten when we started picking the asparagus. It was rewarding to find those delectable spears—some obvious, others nearly hidden in the grass. I became happily engrossed in my task.

My feeling of exhilaration was short-lived, as I had temporarily forgotten that asparagus grows best where cattle have been grazing. Having neglected to watch where I was stepping, I had plopped a boot in the middle of what we midwesterners commonly refer to as a "cow pie." The odor accompanied me to the nearest puddle of water where I sloshed around until the worst of my problem was solved.

When we finally got back to the car, we learned that my husband had gone off on his own, leaving Ted to pick a nearby pasture with Roz and me. At this point, I should mention that we had been told we wouldn't need permission to enter an area unless it was posted with a "No Trespassing" sign. The natives realize that the more often asparagus is harvested the better it grows.

There was no need to cross a ditch this time as a road and culvert had been built to give the rancher access to his land. There was a gate, but I failed to see a way to open it and the barbed wire was too tight to allow us to crawl over or between. I demonstrated to my friends how to lie flat on their backs and inch their way carefully under the bottom wire. Both of them passed their buckets to me and managed, with some difficulty, to get through and regain their footing. We filled our pails with asparagus and returned to the car, using the same method to exit the pasture as we had used to enter it.

As we were unloading our asparagus into the cooler in the back of the station wagon, we saw my husband coming across the pasture we had just left. When he reached the gate, he lifted a wire from around a wooden post, pushed the gate open, and walked through. I could think of no good way to explain to my friends why they had been required to drag themselves bodily over grass and dirt when the gate would have opened so easily.

My husband drove the station wagon onto a shady lane just off the main road where we ate the picnic lunches we had brought. Soon after lunch, we decided it was time to start the long trip home. We found a small café en route where we had a cool drink after changing clothes in their rest rooms.

A few days after our memorable day in the country, I noticed some itchy blisters on my right arm, which could only have been caused by poison ivy. We had made sure our friends could identify the noxious weed and had warned them to avoid it at any cost. I checked with them and neither had a single blister. The "novices" had survived the trip unscathed while I had fallen into a ditch full of water, got cut on a barbed-wire fence, stepped in manure, failed to open a gate, and touched poison ivy.

Our search for wild asparagus has become an annual event, but there have been some changes since that first trip several years ago. We spend less time walking fence rows and more time watching wildlife. Ted has found a way to attach his bucket to a walking stick and Roz sometimes brings her knitting. I have learned to give fewer instructions and pay more attention to my own actions, so far with favorable results.

We all hope to be back in the sandhills next spring with our buckets, coolers, lunches, and repellents. In a world of changing fortunes, this special day in the country has become a valuable constant—sometimes challenging, and always rewarding. After all, the very best treasures are rarely found in the goal itself, but rather in the experience of the hunt.

JEAN SCHNEIDER

HAWAII UNPLUGGED

I've heard it said that your entire life flashes before you when you are about to die. It's true. All of my fifty-two years fast-forwarded that December afternoon as I lay counting the ceiling tiles of the Honolulu International Airport Emergency Clinic.

Our holiday trip began well. My husband, Tim, and I were joining friends in Hawaii to celebrate our thirtieth wedding anniversary. Before boarding, I remembered I needed earplugs. At the nearest counter in the Atlanta airport, I tried to purchase the Ear Planes I used when flying. The only earplugs available were those intended for children. Tim said, "You have small ears. I'll bet they work fine."

Flattered at having small ears, I made my purchase and happily settled into the Delta aisle seat. On take-off the earplugs worked well. When we reached cruising altitude, I removed them since they had little blue plastic antennae. I didn't want to look weird in front of strangers propelled hundreds of miles an hour at 35,000 feet. The stewardess brought the hamster rations passing for dinner. Undaunted, Tim and I toasted our anniversary and limited our trips to the broom closet bathroom. However, ten hours is a long time.

We had our usual discussion on how air travel has changed, how it no longer is a glamorous experience, and reminisced over past luxury flights. Tim said to a fellow traveler, "Air travel is a bus ride in the sky with peanuts." On this trip just for fun, we didn't pay the $5 for the earphones, but made up our own dialogue to the in-flight movie. Some of the other passengers even joined in. A few hours later after working the crossword and reading the airline magazine cover to cover, the pilot announced we were ready to land. I dutifully inserted my earplugs, fastened my seat belt, and put my tray in the upright position.

As the wheels touched down on the asphalt, the air pressure in the cabin changed. My ears popped, but it wasn't until later that I realized that my earplugs had been sucked deep into my ear canal. The pressure, pain, and panic drowned all my excitement of landing in paradise.

I scrambled for my purse and a mirror. My adrenaline pumped. I managed to force the left earplug out. I cocked my head and strained to see the right ear. No sign of the blue tips. The jet taxied to a stop where our friends were waiting to give us the traditional Hawaiian greeting of a kiss and flower lei.

Flushed with a combination of embarrassment and pain, we headed to the Emergency Clinic. Dragging our luggage down ramps and stairs, we finally located a tiny room labeled "Clinic." After ringing the bell and waiting, we were directed to another location. Finally, a thinly built man of Polynesian extraction opened a "speakeasy" window and admitted us inside.

I sat in a chair with a curtain dividing the waiting room from the examining room. The paramedic's hands trembled as he turned my face to look in the ear canal. I didn't have to know Hawaiian to feel the prognosis was not good. When I heard him say the word "hospital," my nurse friend, Sue, went into action.

"Sheila, do you trust me?"

"Yes." I felt the tears coming close to the surface.

"Don't move. I have a needle. I'm going to remove the plug. I can see it but the tweezers aren't long enough. Are you okay with that?"

My eyes answered. With one swift motion, Sue plunged the hypodermic needle into the rubber earplug and pulled it out. I hugged Sue and wiped the tears. I could hear again!

When friends have asked about our thirtieth anniversary trip to Hawaii, I've described the silvery sands edged with black coral, the coffee and macadamia plantations we visited on the way to Kilauea Volcanic National Park, and a ride on the "sugar train" through the cane fields. Of course I'd never leave out swaying coconut palms at sunset or the dancers at the Hula Grill. But the first thing I've said is that I was "unplugged in Hawaii." They always nod and think they understand.

SHEILA S. HUDSON

MORE CHOCOLATE STORIES?

Do you have a short story you want published that fits the spirit of *Chocolate for a Woman's Dreams* or *Chocolate for a Woman's Soul*? I am planning future editions using a similar format that will feature love stories, divine moments, family highlights, overcoming obstacles, following our intuition, and humorous events that teach us to laugh at ourselves. I am seeking heartwarming stories of two to four pages in length that feed your soul.

I invite you to join me in these future projects by sending your special story for consideration. If your story is selected, you will be paid $100 and be listed as a contributing author, and you'll have a biographical paragraph about you included. For more information, or to send a story, please contact:

Kay Allenbaugh
P. O. Box 2165
Lake Oswego, Oregon 97035
kay@allenbaugh.com

For more information, please visit my Web site!
www.chocolateforwomen.com

CONTRIBUTORS

MARY M. ALWARD lives with her husband in southern Ontario, Canada. She has had her work published in both print venues and online. She is presently contributing to *Listening to the Animal,* a series published by *Guideposts.* She has a grown daughter and two beautiful grandsons, whom she spends a lot of time with when she isn't writing. (519) 752-3819. dalward@sprint.ca

MELANIE ANDERSON-CASTER left the cold office of her marketing communications career to stay home full-time with her two children, Tyler and Megan. She now writes out of her warm, cozy home office in Lake of the Pines, California, with her trusty space heater at her side. She is currently working on her first novel, *Behind Closed Doors.* writemel@ips.net

LINDA ASPENSON-BERGSTROM is a former newspaper editor and journalist. She lives the rural life outside of Cumberland, Wisconsin, with her husband, Jeff, and their two kids, Hannah and Beau. She enjoys animals, gardening, and playing with her family. She works as a freelance artist and writer. lindapaints@hotmail.com

GLORIA ATTAR is a writer and journalist from the Midwest, currently living out her dream in Bologna, Italy, with her young daughter. She is a former publicist, seminar leader, and paralegal and is working on her forthcoming novel set in Italy. Her next dream is to own a villa and divide her time between Chicago and Italy. gloriagattar@libero.it

BETTY AUCHARD is a semiretired public school art teacher. Before becoming a writer in 1999, her specialty was the art of printing and dyeing fabric. Her instructions and artwork have appeared in periodicals and books since 1974. *Making Journals by Hand,* released in July 2000, features her six leaf-printed travel journals. She is also an active member of the International Nature Printing Society. She is presently working full time on her memoir stories for future publication. btauchard@aol.com

URSULA BACON fled Nazi Germany with her parents and spent the next nine years in China. She was interned along with 18,000 European refugees by Japanese occupation forces in Shanghai for four years. She emigrated to the United States at the end of WWII. Ursula is married to author Thorn Bacon, and they operate a small publishing house and write books. She is the coauthor of *Savage Shadows* (New Horizon, New York) and the author of *The Nervous Hostess Cookbook,* March 1996. (503) 682-9821

MARGO BALLANTYNE has a master's degree in Art History and is a Visual Resource Curator at Lewis & Clark College in Portland, Oregon. This is her first attempt at publishing on a subject other than art, although she has "performed" her stories for her indulgent family and friends for years. She is a founding member of the "Wobble City Hikers" and fosters a dream of, one day, owning a small organic herb farm with her husband, Glenn.

JENNIFER BROWN BANKS is founder and president of a community-based arts organization located in the Chicago area. She is a feature writer for *Being Single* magazine and a public relations office manager. Her publishing credits include *Today's Black Woman Magazine, Chicago Sun-Times, Today's Chicago Woman, Just for Black*

Men, Gospel Synergy, and several Chocolate sequels. She was recently recognized by Marquis's *Who's Who in America.* (773) 509-8018

SANDE BORITZ BERGER began writing as a young teenager because her letters amused her parents and "they finally heard me." For several years she got sidetracked in the corporate world writing and producing promotional video programs, until finally returning to her passion. A poet, essayist, and fiction writer, her work appears in *Every Woman Has a Story,* by Warner Books, and in *Cup of Comfort,* Adams Media. She has completed a novel about a seventies young woman's boredom in suburbia and its consequences. She lives on Long Island and Manhattan with her "first reader" husband, Steven, and has two extremely independent hardworking daughters. MurphyFace@aol.com

DIANE GONZALES BERTRAND lives in San Antonio, Texas, where she is Writer-in-Residence at St. Mary's University. Her bilingual picture books for children include *The Last Doll, Family, Familia,* and *Sip, Slurp, Soup, Soup,* all published by Arte Publico Press (Houston, Texas). She visits schools in Texas, Florida, and Colorado, reading to children and sharing her love of writing with them. "True Rewards" is her fourth published essay in the Chocolate series. dbertrand@stmarytx.edu

VALENTINA A. BLOOMFIELD is a receptionist and switchboard operator who truly enjoys her job. She has been published in *Chocolate for a Teen's Soul* and *Chocolate for a Woman's Blessings.* She hopes in the future to write a children's book. She's had stories published in her local newspaper and her poetry has been published also. She's a member of the National Library of Poetry, and MADD (Mothers Against Drunk Driving). She donates her free time to helping others and volunteers for the Make-A-Wish Foundation and Love Letters. Her husband, Keith, and stepdaughter,

Jennifer, reside with her in Vacaville, California (707) 451-2490. Bloooomers@aol.com

DEBRA AYERS BROWN has inspirational stories in *Guideposts*, the *Chocolate* series, *Chicken Soup*, and *From Eulogy to Joy*. She is marketing director for Savannah Technical College and an IBO with Quixtar, an Internet-based company. She is a Southeastern Writer's Association board member, a graduate of the University of Georgia, and has a master's in Business Administration. dabmlb@clds.net

RENIE SZILAK BURGHARDT, who was born in Hungary and came to the United States in 1951, is a freelance writer. Some publications in which her work has appeared are *Angels on Earth*, *Mature Living*, *Fate*, *Cat Fancy*, *Midwest Living*, *Nostalgia*, *The Friend*, and others. She resides in Doniphan, Missouri. Renie@clnet.net

MICHELE WALLACE CAMPANELLI enjoys the part she's playing in creating a national best-selling *Chocolate* series. She lives on the space coast of Florida with her husband, Louis. She is a graduate of Writer's Digest School and Keiser College. Author of *Hero of Her Heart*, published by Blue Note Books, and *Margarita, Keeper of the Shroud*, published by Hollis Books, she finds writing to be her outlet for artistic expression. Currently she is working on the sequel to *Keeper of the Shroud*, short stories, and a movie deal. www.michelecampanelli.com

TALIA CARNER is a novelist with three yet-to-be-published novels. Her theme is motherhood threatened by big government. Before writing full time, she founded Business Women Marketing Corporation, a consulting firm whose clients were Fortune 500 companies, and was the publisher of *Savvy Woman* magazine. Active in women's civic and professional organizations, she teaches entrepreneurial skills to women and participated in the NGO women's conference in Beijing in 1995. Israeli-born, she served in the Israeli army during the 1967 Six-Day War. She and her husband and four children live in Long Island, New York. TalYof@aol.com

MITZI CHANDLER is a published writer and inspirational speaker on the subject of alcoholism, codependency, and child abuse. Her books *Whiskey's Song* and *Gentle Reminders for Codependents* focus on the trauma experienced by children in an alcoholic home and the recovery process. She worked as a nurse/counselor in alcohol rehab centers in Chicago and St. Louis. Her spare time is spent playing and growing with her three cherished grandchildren. (821) 661-7415

KATHLEEN HILLIARD COYNE, Ed.D., is presently teaching at Lockwood Elementary School in Bothell, Washington (Northshore School District). She also serves as an adjunct education professor at Seattle University. She was the recipient of the Christa McAuliffe Award for Excellence in Education in Washington State. She and her husband, Dr. Robert Coyne, are speakers and published authors on the topic of building positive character within schools. (425) 489-6328. CannonBKMJ@aol.com

BARBARA DAVEY is an executive director at Christ Hospital in Jersey City, New Jersey, where she is responsible for public relations and fundraising. She holds bachelor's and master's degrees in English from Seton Hall University. A service near to her heart is the "Look Good, Feel Better" program, which supplies complimentary wigs and cosmetics to women undergoing treatment for cancer. Her attitude toward life is "expect a miracle!" She and her husband, Reinhold Becker, live in Verona, New Jersey. wisewords2@aol.com

MARILYN D. DAVIS lives, writes, and works in the Chicago area. Her short stories, humor pieces, and first-person essays have appeared in local publications and on various Web sites. She holds a bachelor's and master's degree in Education, and has worked in teaching and administrative capacities at various levels, from preschool to college. In her spare time, she enjoys collecting fossil crinoids on the beaches of southwest Michigan. She is married and the mother of two school-age boys, who make her grateful every day for her sense of humor. www.allshewrites.com

JENNIFER DOBRENSKI has been teaching elementary school since 1996. She is currently teaching internationally and lives with her husband in Basel, Switzerland. Previously, she has worked with severely handicapped children through community programs such as Easter Seals. She is still involved in community youth work and one day hopes to teach visually impaired children.

BETH DUNCAN is an avid writer and has set a goal to empower as many women as possible through personal contact, her short stories, and a book of poetry on which she is currently working. She lives in North Carolina with her three children, two of whom are in college. gingerfreeze11@usa.net

CANDIS FANCHER, M.S. C.C.C. in Speech Pathology, is the founder of Inner Sources. Audiences are inspired by her upbeat philosophy. Her "Pleasure Pause" seminars have energized participants to adopt more positive lifestyles. Her "Staying Afloat in the Stresspools of Life" seminars explore practical ideas for integrating humor into your personal and professional life. Her "SNAC" approach provides practical and humorous ways for *Stopping, Noticing, Acting* and *Creating* heart-to-heart connections. She is also a speech/voice coach and is a member of the American Speech-Language Hearing Association and the National Speakers Association. (952) 890-3897

SUSAN FARR-FAHNCKE is a freelance writer living in Utah. She writes for inspirational books and magazines and runs a Web site and daily list of inspirational stories. She has recently published her book *Angel's Legacy,* a tribute to her inspiring sister who lost her battle with a brain tumor. Susan@2theheart.com. www.2THEHEART.com

KRISTI FRAHM recently resigned from her high school English instructor position in order to spend more time with her husband, Donn, and her two children, Whitney and Kendall. Born and raised in North Dakota, she loves the transitions among the four distinct seasons that the state has to offer. She enjoys traveling, eating in unique restaurants, watching sentimental movies, and reading fictional short stories and novels, along with the *Chocolate* series of books, of course! defrahm@stellarnet.com

LUCI N. FULLER has essays and short stories that have appeared in gift books, anthologies, and newspapers around the country. She lives in Gresham, Oregon and is currently at work on a book-length work of fiction. (503) 492-4317. LuciFuller@aol.com

JAYNE GARRETT serves as a business/personal coach and facilitator professionally. She writes lyrics, poems, and stories for children and adults. She writes from the heart while interspersing humor into her work. Her greatest joy and inspiration come from her family, friends, and God. FOCUSunltd@aol.com

JENNIFER GORDON GRAY has worked as a writer, editor, and photographer in the newspaper industry since 1983, and as a correspondent for several publications serving members and friends of Soka Gakkai International. She recently enjoyed a six-month writing odyssey at Howeford Cottage in northern Scotland. She loves hiking, snowshoeing, and hugging her cat, Bear. TartanPony@Juno.com. http://TartanPony.Homestead.com

ALICIA WILDE HARDING lives with her husband and three children in Massachusetts. She is delighted to be a member of the *Chocolate* sisterhood. She has been published previously in *Pandemonium or Life with Kids* and *I Killed June Cleaver*. She is currently working on a romance/mystery novel. mah608hmh@aol.com

KATHIE HARRINGTON holds a master's degree in Speech Pathology from Truman State University. She is engaged in private practice in Las Vegas, Nevada, and is an international speaker. She has authored four books in the field of speech pathology and numerous short stories and poems. As a thirty-year-old young adult, Doug is employed full time in the housekeeping department at one of the premiere resorts in the world, the Venetian on the Las Vegas Strip. He attended the University of Nevada Las Vegas for two years in their special programs. Doug drives his new car, works on the World Wide Web, and lives at home. (702) 435-8748; fax: (702) 436-9161. TappyH@aol.com

LANA ROBERTSON HAYES, who has an M.A. in Education, is the author of many humorous essays, articles, and greeting cards. A former teacher, she wields her pen at life's absurdities, which she finds amusing, and her family's antics, which strike her as hilarious. A transplanted Southerner, she now lives in Arizona but still misses her native state of Georgia. BritishTea@aol.com

LAVONNE HOLLAND owns her own salon in Lake Oswego, Oregon.

SHEILA S. HUDSON, Bright Ideas founder, is a freelance writer, speaker, and wife/mother/grandmother. Her credits include *Chocolate for a Teen's Soul, Chocolate for a Woman's Blessing, Chocolate for a Woman's Heart, God's Vitamin C for the Spirit of Men, Taking Education Higher, Casas por Cristo: Stories from the Border, Life's Little*

Rule Book, and *From Eulogy to Joy.* She is a frequent contributor to *Christian Standard, Lookout, The Athens Magazine* and *Athens Parent.* (706) 546-5085. sheila-brightideas@home.com.www.sheila-bright ideas.com

BETSY HUMPHREYS is a freelancer who writes creative nonfiction and poetry based on her North Carolina foothills home and suitcase experiences.

BETH BOSWELL JACKS has work that has been accepted for publication in a number of magazines, including *Ladybug, Hopscotch, Shining Star, Kids' Highway, Boys' Quest, Lighthouse Story Collections, Working Writer, The Balanced Woman, Lonzie's Fried Chicken, Devo'zine, Story Mates, Story Friends,* and *U.S. Kids.* A weekly personal essay columnist for the *Cleveland* (Mississippi) *Bolivar Commercial,* she has also published one book of creative nonfiction—*Grit, Guts, and Baseball*—a story of sports and race relations in the Mississippi Delta. A full member of the Society of Children's Book Writers and Illustrators, she lives with her husband and basset hound in Cleveland, Mississippi. jaxgbt@ tecinfo.com

ROBERTA BEACH JACOBSON is the editor of Kafenio (www.kafe-niocom.com), a monthly e-zine focusing on European life and culture. She lives in Greece. editor@kafeniocom.com

BETH SCHORR JAFFE is the author of the novel *Fade to Blue* (not yet published). She's completed a second novel and a collection of short stories and has signed with a literary agent in New York City. Born and raised in Brooklyn, New York, she graduated from Brooklyn College with a B.A. in English Literature/Creative Writing. She now lives in New Jersey with her husband and two sons. Writr2b838@aol.com

PHYLLIS JAMISON worked as a secretary for years while raising her two daughters. She entered college at forty and studied journalism. Fiction writing and a study of human nature are her primary loves, and now that she is retired, she enjoys spending her time in those pursuits. She's had three poems published recently and is currently writing a novel concerning a midlife crisis in the marriage of a middle-aged couple. She also works as a mental health volunteer counseling older women suffering from depression. She lives in Beaverton, Oregon. (503) 644-8691.

PAMELA JENKINS lives with her husband, Stanley, and their four children on a small farm outside of Henryetta, Oklahoma. She is the office manager of her husband's veterinary practice, and they are avid supporters of 4-H and FFA youth activities. She also owns a rabbitry and raises pedigreed red Satin rabbits. Working with animals and children in a small, hometown environment gives her the inspiration for many of her stories.

AMY LYNNE JOHNSON is a past contributor to the *Chocolate* series. She's a writer living in Sarasota, Florida, where she is currently working on books for children as well as several volunteer projects. AmyJ97209@aol.com

TAYLOR JOSEPH lives in Florida with her husband of twenty-five years. They marked their recent anniversary with a ceremonial renewal of their wedding vows. Sharing their story with *Chocolate* readers is her way of expressing the gratitude she holds in her heart for the gift of a good man. She is a co-owner of Grandfeather Productions, a group of writers whose mission is to connect with the isolated, to comfort the injured, and to caution the innocent. Grandfeather@cs.com

CINDY KAUFFMAN lives in Green, Ohio, with her husband and four children. She has authored a weekly humor column there since 1996. Generally unencumbered by any lack of material, her biggest challenge in meeting deadline day is finding time in which to write, and sanity with which to do it. CinKau75@aol.com

ELIZABETH KRENIK is the mother of three daughters and a fourth grade teacher. She writes a monthly book review column for her local newspaper and has published short stories in newspapers and books. She is a public speaker for the Minnesota AIDS Project and currently is presenting readings of a play she has written about her brother, who died as a result of the virus that causes AIDS. She has acted in and directed community theater productions over the last twelve years. She considers her role as mother the most important one in life. She enjoys spending time with her family and friends, gardening, reading, sketching, traveling, and working on building projects in and around her home in Le Center, Minnesota. etrax@frontiernet.net

EDNA MINER LARSON is a published writer of poems and short stories. She started working as a salesperson, then a stenographer, bookkeeper, and when she retired, she was the administrative director of a large physicians' exchange. Her college education was wedged in along the way. Since retirement, she has enjoyed creating and teaching the art of Eggery. She has also taught a literacy program through a local college and has worked as a hospice volunteer. Her family and friends tell her she's always been a writer and her success in being published is about to make a believer of her.

BEVERLY C. LUCEY is an instructor of education at Agnes Scott College as well as a writer whose work has appeared in numerous magazines and e-zines. Her stories "Gift Wrap" (July 2000) and "Scissors, Paper, Rock" (January 2001) have been published in *Zoetrope All Story Extra Magazine* and "Waiting for the Flight," published in the *Vestal Review* (Summer 2000), has been nominated for a Pushcart Prize. In addition, she has also had fiction published in *Portland Maine Magazine, Flint River Review* (1999), and *Moxie* (Winter 2000). Four of her stories are anthologized in *We Teach Them All* (Stenhouse Press, 1996). WordsNest@aol.com

DENA MCCLUNG lives in Aurora, Colorado, and works for the Federal Aviation Administration as an air traffic controller at a major airport. She enjoys flying, playing piano, writing, and exploring the great outdoors. denamccl@pcez.com

CLAUDIA MCCORMICK is a freelance writer and member of the Dublin, California, city council. She and her husband, Tom, have a combined family of six children, eleven grandchildren, and four stray cats. Chindidub@aol.com

ELEANOR MCLAUGHLIN lives in British Columbia, Canada, and is a sign language interpreter for the deaf. She and her husband, Joe, of twenty years have three teenage sons. She is a Catholic, and her passions include meditation and writing. EleanorMcL@aol.com

RENE B. MELTON is a working mom, wife, and chocolate lover. This is her first contribution, and she is thrilled to share her story with readers. Her time is split between her seventeen-year career, her husband of eighteen years, two boys, one cat, one dog, PTA, and Little League.

MOLLY MEYERS is a retired correction officer and a writer. She has a B.A. (cum laude) in English with a minor in journalism and is pursuing an M.F.A. in Writing Studies. She enjoys riding/jumping horses, fencing, and sentimental movies. She is currently working on her memoirs and believes her inspiration comes from the silent stirring that resides in us all. (973) 427-8675

AMY MUNNELL has been a freelance writer/editor since 1987. Her work has been featured in such magazines as *Byline, Careers and the disABLED, Georgia Journal,* and *Athens Magazine.* She is on the Board of Directors for the Southeastern Writers Association. She lives in Athens, Georgia. (706) 354-0361. nega writer@ yahoo.com

CAROL TOKAR PAVLISKA is a mother of three children, who provide her with endless material for her passion of writing. She and her husband, Jeff, have been married for sixteen years and live on the family farm in Floresville, Texas, where Carol pens a local newspaper column called "Kidz-n-Tow."

FELICE R. PRAGER is a freelance writer from Scottsdale, Arizona. After successful careers in education and retail management, she threw in the towel a few years ago to do what she loves best: write. Her work has since appeared in a number of national and local publications, as well as in a number of e-zines. FelPrager@aol. com. www.1derfulwords.com

LILLIAN QUASCHNICK is originally from Fresno, California, where she taught foreign language at the high school level. She currently resides in San Lorenzo, California, and is teaching in the Bay Area. She is an associate editor/author of a textbook on the California raisin industry to be published this year, and is in the process of writing about growing up Italian-American. lmg1450@greaterbaynet.com

LISA ROBERTSON began writing at the urging of her parents, who believed they saw a bit of talent in her holiday newsletters. After fifteen years of working in the veterinary field, she is now a stay-at-home mom, writing stories of her life experiences and those of her two children. Along with her husband and kids, she shares her life with four cats and a work-in-progress English garden at her Pacific Northwest home. b4bastet@juno.com

JUDI SADOWSKY is a writer who has done television and magazine work. She has been married for thirty-five years to the love of her life and has two fabulous children and one amazing daughter-in-law. She is currently working on a book of essays and patiently waiting for her first grandchild to be conceived. jsadowsky@earthlink.net

MARY SASS, M.A. in Counseling, is a writer, artist, lecturer, and former teacher, who has published many essays, short stories, and articles about writing. Her radio scripts and television documentaries have won awards. She has also won awards for her oil paintings, exhibiting in juried one-woman and group shows. She has written novels and illustrated a Christmas novella, *The Katy Ornament*. A member of Mystery Writers of America and the MWA Speaker's Bureau, she is listed in *Who's Who of American Women, Who's Who of the Midwest,* and *Who's Who in Entertainment.* (847) 674-7118, and (616) 432-4466 June–September.

HOLLY NOELLE SCHAEFER, a business systems engineer, says she realizes that sometimes life hits you head-on, like a Mack truck. During the past year, she was rear-ended twice, transferred to a new job, lost four friendships, had a stroke, discovered that her husband was having an affair with one of her best friends, and started divorce proceedings. At that point, she decided to either write or to run away to Paris. She lives with her six-year-old daughter, True Noelle Saenz, in St. Anthony Village, Minnesota. She is currently working on a collection of short stories. Just in case, she keeps an Air France plane schedule in her purse at all times. hollyschaefer@yahoo.com

JEAN SCHNEIDER is retired and lives with her husband, Bob, in York, Nebraska. She has been published in *NebraskaLand Magazine* and writes primarily to record a family history for her four grandsons. (402) 362-4778. rs83256@alltel.net

LEIGH SENTER has had four short stories published in literary magazines. She has had dozens of poems and pen-and-ink drawings published in magazines as varied as *Lonzies Fried Chicken, Sow's Ear Poetry Review,* and *Limestone Circle. The Urban Hiker* occasionally prints her thoughts on everything from diets to religion. She lives at Purnell Crossroads in North Carolina with two teenaged daughters, Doc Watson, the dog, and several goldfish.

SHELLEY SIGMAN is a freelance writer and photographer who, after twenty-one years heading her own landscape design company, traded her T-square for the tools of writing. She is an entertainment reporter for the *Main Line Times* in suburban Philadelphia and former lifestyle feature writer and restaurant columnist for Gannett Newspapers. She's had articles, humor and fiction, featured in the *Chicago Tribune, Philadelphia's Exponent, Green's Magazine,* and *Reader's Break.* siggie@enter.net

LIBBY SIMON, M.S.W., is a freelance writer living in Winnipeg, Manitoba. She has worked for twenty years as a school clinician and parent educator. Her articles and books include bibliotherapy for children and families, articles on social/educational issues, personal narratives, and humor. She has been published in newspapers, magazines, and scholarly journals in the United States and Canada and has developed a violence prevention program for K–3 called "Don't Fight, It's Not Right." For further information (204) 334-7180. libby@escape.ca

CAROL L. SKOLNICK writes humor, personal essays, and performance text, in addition to her award-winning work in creative marketing. Her writings have appeared in *Glamour, The Sun: A Magazine of Ideas, The English Journal, DM News,* and on the Web sites mx.Aprimo.com, Writer Online, and Themestream.com. New York audiences enjoyed her two-character play *Hopelessly Devoted* as part of Love Creek Productions' One-Act Festival in 1996. She lives and works in New York City's historic Greenwich Village. sput6@aol.com.

SHEILA STEPHENS is an international award-winning poet, writing teacher, columnist, and speaker, who enjoys helping people build their lives "from the inside, out." To her, self-esteem is a spiritual journey of accepting the seed of love that divine spirit places in each heart. She has just completed *Walking with the Flowers: 50 Weeks of Quiet Meditations for a Woman's Busy World.* Her professional services include Creativity Coaching; personalized Correspondence Writing Classes (available worldwide); and "Walking with the Flowers" Seminars. joywriters@uswest.net

LEA C. TARTANIAN is a medical secretary, writer, a member of Toastmasters, and has written for over twenty-two publications. She has also published devotionals in three books: *Treasures of a Woman's Heart* and *Seasons of a Woman's Heart* by Lynne Morrissey, and *More God's Abundance* by Kathy Collard Miller. Her goals are to publish inspirational books, conduct journaling workshops, and be an inspirational speaker. She resides in Endwell, New York. (607) 754-3671. dtartani@stny.rr.com

GERALDINE (GERRY) TRICKLE balances write-for-business projects with creating fiction and nonfiction. She is a published author of personal essays. Her writing voice speaks with the wisdom gained from navigating the rocky shoals of Love and Loss, surviving the Straits of Single Parenting, and sailing in Relationship

Regatas. Today, she frequently drops anchor in Grand-children Bay, then heads back to New Jersey to tend to a novel-in-progress. gtworks@home.com. www.writer-online.com

CATHERINE VAUGHAN-OBREGON is a full-time English Instructor at Redlands East Valley High School, Running Springs, California, and she teaches part-time at California State University San Bernardino in the Education Department. She has a B.A. in English, a master's in Secondary Education, and a Concentration in Communications. She writes for her own catharsis. obesecret@aol.com

LINDA H. WATERMAN is a successful freelance proofreader who finally decided to do some writing of her own. Born in Connecticut, she has traveled the world and spent a life-changing year living in Rome, Italy. Today she resides in California where she tries to perpetuate a Mediterranean lifestyle—while writing what she hopes are amusing essays. LINDAWAT@aol.com

TAMMY WILSON was introduced to political discussions at the family dinner table, and she has followed American politics ever since. After attending colleges in Illinois and England, she earned a journalism degree from the University of Missouri and became a reporter for the nation's smallest daily, the *Shelbyville Daily Union*. She has since worked as a business writer/editor and her works have appeared in several journals. She makes her home in North Carolina.

MARY ZELINKA lives with her springer spaniel, Molly McGee (aka Wild Thing), in Albany, Oregon, where she is the program director for the Center Against Rape and Domestic Violence. There she works to empower survivors to break the cycle of abuse and to rebuild their lives free from violence. Her work has appeared in *Chocolate for a Lover's Heart* and *Chocolate for a Teen's Heart*. She actively seeks and finds magic everywhere and has been described as being "chronically idealistic." She still misses Beau, who had to be put to sleep in 1988. maryz@proaxis.com

LYNNE LAYTON ZIELINSKI rakes leaves and rearranges yard rocks in Huntsville, Alabama. A freelance writer, Lynne believes that life is a gift from God, and what we do with it is our gift to God. She has a seventeenth-century historical novel in progress. (256) 883-1592. Arisway@aol.com

ACKNOWLEDGMENTS

My heartfelt thanks to the *Chocolate* Sisters for offering their delightful, uplifting true stories about making their dreams come true. Many of the ways that we discover our heart's desires are captured in these pages thanks to them.

My continued heartfelt gratitude to my agent, Peter Miller of PMA Literary and Film Management, Inc., and his team of dream weavers for making my wishes come true.

And to all the talented chocolate lovers at Fireside/Simon & Schuster, from senior editor, Caroline Sutton, to those in the Marketing, Sales, and Special Sales departments, I greatly appreciate all that you do for the *Chocolate* series!

To my family, friends, and administrative support staff, may your dreams be fulfilled and always exceed your expectations.

I treasure all of you.

ABOUT THE AUTHOR

Kay Allenbaugh is the author of *Chocolate for a Woman's Soul, Chocolate for a Woman's Heart; Chocolate for a Lover's Heart; Chocolate for a Mother's Heart, Chocolate for a Woman's Spirit, Chocolate for a Teen's Soul, Chocolate for a Woman's Blessings,* and *Chocolate for a Teen's Heart.* She resides in Lake Oswego, Oregon, with her husband, Eric Allenbaugh, author of *Wake-Up Calls: You Don't Have to Sleepwalk Through Your Life, Love or Career!*